Palgrave Executive Essentials

Today's complex and changing business environment brings with it a number of pressing challenges. To be successful, business professionals are increasingly required to leverage and spot future trends, be masters of strategy, all while leading responsibly, inspiring others, mastering financial techniques and driving innovation.

Palgrave Executive Essentials empowers you to take your skills to the next level. Offering a suite of resources to support you on your executive journey and written by renowned experts from top business schools, the series is designed to support professionals as they embark on executive education courses, but it is equally applicable to practicing leaders and managers. Each book brings you in-depth case studies, accompanying video resources, reflective questions, practical tools and core concepts that can be easily applied to your organization, all written in an engaging, easy to read style.

George S. Day

# Innovate to Grow

Gaining and Sustaining a Growth Advantage

George S. Day
University of Pennsylvania
Philadelphia, PA, USA

ISSN 2731-5614   ISSN 2731-5622 (electronic)
Palgrave Executive Essentials
ISBN 978-3-031-77672-4   ISBN 978-3-031-77673-1 (eBook)
https://doi.org/10.1007/978-3-031-77673-1

© The Editor(s) (if applicable) and The Author(s), under exclusive license to Springer Nature Switzerland AG 2025

This work is subject to copyright. All rights are solely and exclusively licensed by the Publisher, whether the whole or part of the material is concerned, specifically the rights of translation, reprinting, reuse of illustrations, recitation, broadcasting, reproduction on microfilms or in any other physical way, and transmission or information storage and retrieval, electronic adaptation, computer software, or by similar or dissimilar methodology now known or hereafter developed.
The use of general descriptive names, registered names, trademarks, service marks, etc. in this publication does not imply, even in the absence of a specific statement, that such names are exempt from the relevant protective laws and regulations and therefore free for general use.
The publisher, the authors and the editors are safe to assume that the advice and information in this book are believed to be true and accurate at the date of publication. Neither the publisher nor the authors or the editors give a warranty, expressed or implied, with respect to the material contained herein or for any errors or omissions that may have been made. The publisher remains neutral with regard to jurisdictional claims in published maps and institutional affiliations.

This Palgrave Macmillan imprint is published by the registered company Springer Nature Switzerland AG
The registered company address is: Gewerbestrasse 11, 6330 Cham, Switzerland

If disposing of this product, please recycle the paper.

# Acknowledgments

Progress toward understanding how innovation delivers faster organic growth comes when practice illuminates theory, and vice versa. If theory and practice are the two piers holding up the ends of a bridge, then research strengthens the deck that spans these piers. The field research supporting this book illuminates how growth leaders achieve and sustain a faster rate of growth.

This book is the result of my thirty years of collaborating closely with many growth-leading companies in various roles: as a team member of their innovation projects, as a facilitator of their strategy deliberations, as a designer and teacher of their executive programs, and as a member of their Boards of Directors. I am very grateful for what I learned from the talented executive teams of firms such as Medtronic, Mastercard, Merck, Novartis, IBM, GE Aircraft Engines, W. L. Gore & Associates, and DuPont. These and other growth leaders have inspired and provoked me to understand them more deeply. My second debt of gratitude is to the Marketing Science Institute that provides a bridge between leaders in industry and academia.

I have been very fortunate to be on the faculty of the Wharton School of the University of Pennsylvania, where ambidexterity is valued and encouraged. This book would not have been possible without the continuing support of the Mack Institute for Innovation Management, whose mission is to advance the practice of innovation in organizations. I'm especially grateful for the encouragement of Harbir Singh and Valery

Yakubovitch. This innovative hub in a knowledge network has been generously supported by Bill Mack, for which I am very grateful.

I have also benefited from the insights shared by the colleagues in my extended network, including Dave Reibstein, Charles Baden-Fuller, Kaihan Krippendorf, Michael Taylor, Eric Langshur, Mette Lauresen, and so many others that have influenced my thinking. It is a particular pleasure to acknowledge my close friend and long-time collaborator Paul Schoemaker who has influenced and informed my thinking about strategy and how to profit from uncertainty. Tom Donaldson is both a friend and an exemplar of rigorous thinking. Of course, these colleagues are not at all responsible for how I have used their ideas and approaches.

A writing journey benefits from the sponsorship and encouragement of a thoughtful editor. I greatly appreciate the confidence, support, and insights of my editor Marcus Ballenger at Palgrave Macmillan. Throughout the writing process, Erika Burnett kept the manuscript moving forward with skill and unfailing good cheer.

This book is dedicated to my wonderful and loving wife Alice, who supported me throughout this project.

Villanova, PA  
August 2024

George S. Day

# Praise for *Innovate to Grow*

"This book is an essential read for every CEO and leadership team striving to identify and capitalize on organic growth opportunities without falling into the trap of quick but costly acquisitions. It challenges us to reflect on whether we have the right organizations and leadership teams in place, and how we can build innovation capabilities necessary for sustained growth. It's surprising that a book like this wasn't available sooner, given how many firms have struggled to achieve organic growth."
—Myoung Woo Lee, *Executive Vice Chairman of Dongwon Group, parent of Starkist*

"Companies realize the critical importance of organic innovation to drive growth. But in practice, this tends to be loosely driven, even ad-hoc. There is little clarity on how to drive innovation from within the organization. Instead, inorganic strategies are seen as a quicker route to innovating. The assumption is that innovation can be left to startups and you just invest in them or acquire them. I haven't seen that work very often! George Day brings clarity and fills this gap in driving organic innovation. He combines his research insights with clear frameworks and actionable steps."
—Alok Bardiya, *VC Investor and Board Member*

"George Day masterfully distills the complexity of driving sustainable growth into five critical questions that every leader must answer. His framework of four innovation disciplines, provides a structured approach to overcoming the challenges of organic growth. He sequences these disciplines into an 'innovation flywheel' that turns theory into a practical guide. This book is a must-read for business leaders and innovation managers seeking to unlock the growth potential of their organizations."

—Mohan Sawhney, *Associate Dean of Digital Innovation, Northwestern University*

"George Day continues to challenge corporate executives encumbered by entrenched business models and mindsets with renewed approaches to organic growth fueled by innovation. There is hope for any established company that has the courage to commit to and master the innovation disciplines laid out in this book."

—Scott Snyder, *Chief Digital Officer, Eversana*

"This book will change the way that firms approach organic growth. George Day, with his flair for bringing order to complex strategy arenas, has drawn upon years of observing growth leader firms to develop the four innovation disciplines that your firm can use to turn aspirational growth goals into ongoing reality. This book will transform your firm."

—Dave Aaker, *Vice Chairman at Prophet*

"An easy way to grow is to buy other companies. However, so many firms that adopted the merger and acquisition route performed poorly. I am so pleased that George Day focused his research on organic growth. Every company needs to define and exploit its own natural opportunities. Professor Day, one of America's top marketing and management experts, offers his insights based on years of close observation and consulting experience."

—Philip Kotler, *S.C. Johnson Distinguished Professor of International Marketing, Northwestern University*

"Organic growth is worth many times more than acquired growth, but less than one in five are able deliver it. Day dissects innovation flywheels of those rare companies able to consistently outperform competitors through organic innovation, dissecting what it takes to consistently and sustainably generate innovations that tap emerging technologies to delight customers while generating profits and value to shareholders."

—Kaihan Krippendorf, *Founder of Outhinker Networks a global thinktank*

"*Innovate to Grow* offers a deeply insightful and practical roadmap for those seeking to transform their organizations. George Day's latest work distills decades of experience and cutting-edge research into a compelling narrative. As companies grapple with rapid technological change and rising competitive pressures, Innovate to Grow explores how innovation can become a disciplined, repeatable process. His insights into how firms can capture opportunities earlier than their rivals make this book essential for any organization aiming to achieve and maintain a competitive growth advantage."

—Eric Langshur, *Co-founder and Managing Partner Abundant Venture Partners*

"Managing and sustaining innovation befuddles most firms. All recognize its importance for organic growth, but few have mastered the art. It is not an overstatement to suggest that George Day's new book provides the recipe for corporate leaders to master the innovation art. His four "innovation disciplines" enlivened with myriad illustrations of best innovation practices from leading firms provide corporate leaders the pathway to not only mastering the art of innovation but to winning in our increasingly turbulent environment."

—Liam Fahey, *Partner Leadership Forum*

"In a time when open innovation and innovation ecosystems often sound like buzzwords, "Innovate to Grow" restores a refreshing balance by revisiting the time-tested, foundational principles of innovation. George Day brings clarity and discipline to the conversation, skillfully reinventing a traditional approach for today's interconnected world. By focusing on leadership commitment, strategic choices, and disciplined creativity, alongside collaboration, Day provides a blueprint for sustainable growth. This book is essential reading for leaders who seek not just to follow trends, but to master innovation for the long haul."

—Valery Yakubovich, *Executive Director, Mack Institute for Innovation Management*

"George Day's previous research on strategic vigilance doesn't sit in my bookshelf – it has earned a prime position on my desk. I expect that this new book will find a similar spot on the desks of many CEOs. I wish I had this book years ago, so I could slap it on the desk of every CEO that talked about innovation but never knew how to start."

—Roger Dennis, *Dennis & Partners (Auckland, NZ)*

# Contents

| | | |
|---|---|---|
| 1 | Introduction: Why This Book? Why Now? | 1 |
| 2 | Learning from Growth Leaders | 5 |
| 3 | Demonstrating Leadership Commitment to Innovation | 23 |
| 4 | Strategies for Achieving Growth Ambitions | 39 |
| 5 | Seeking Growth Opportunities | 55 |
| 6 | Deciding Which Opportunities to Capture | 69 |
| 7 | Accomplishing the Work of Innovation | 81 |
| 8 | Turning an Innovation Flywheel Faster | 95 |
| 9 | Sustaining a Growth Advantage | 107 |
| Appendix A: About the Research | | 119 |
| Appendix B: An Innovation Diagnostic | | 121 |
| List of Figures | | 125 |
| End Notes to Innovate to Grow | | 127 |
| Index | | 141 |

CHAPTER 1

# Introduction: Why This Book? Why Now?

A persistent dilemma erodes the ability of most companies to innovate and grow faster than their rivals. Although organic growth tops the leadership agenda of four of five public companies, most leadership teams are dissatisfied with the ability of their organization to innovate. They are regularly frustrated by missing their ambitious goals for top and bottom-line growth from within. This book is an antidote for this costly mismatch between unrealistic organic growth aspirations and an inability to innovate.

Narrowing the gap between aspirations and ability has greater urgency when firms must also keep up with transformative advances in technology, from GenAI and quantum computing to autonomous vehicles and gene editing. These advances promise great opportunities for those able to seize them faster than their rivals. They also magnify uncertainty by blurring market boundaries, raising customer expectations, attracting new competitors, and posing new regulatory issues. With greater uncertainty comes greater opportunity—if a firm can seize it. An apt metaphor for this era of technological ferment is the Japanese character for "crisis"; written by juxtaposing the characters for "danger" and "hidden opportunity."

**Learning from organic growth leaders.** These leaders have mastered four innovation disciplines, working together through their innovation flywheels, to propel them ahead of their rivals. The first innovation discipline is sustained leadership commitment to innovation, demonstrated through consistent investments to ensure their firm has superior innovation talent and capabilities. These commitments are guided by the second discipline of making strategic choices of the growth ambitions for the firm and how their innovation resources are allocated. Growth leaders keep ahead with the third innovation discipline of capturing better growth opportunities sooner than their rivals. They solidify their growth advantage by excelling at the fourth discipline and doing the messy, creative, and risky work of innovation.

In my roles as a strategy consultant, board member, researcher, teacher, and director of executive education programs on innovation, and co-Director of the Mack Institute for Innovation Management at the Wharton School, I'm often asked by senior executives, how their firms can better innovate to grow faster from within. They are seeking answers to their crucial growth questions:

- *How much faster can we grow from within?* This prompts further questions: What are the "bottlenecks" that constrain your growth? What are your ambitions for growth relative to the momentum of your present strategy? What resources can be allocated to innovation activities?
- *Do we have the right organization?* If an innovation culture is software, it runs on the hardware of processes, procedures and structures. Unless a firm is already ambidextrous their organizational hardware is seldom able to support the work of innovation.
- *How can we think about future opportunities when the present devours our attention?* The ability to simultaneously manage today's operations for cash flow, while capitalizing on emergent opportunities to grow, separates the growth leaders from the laggards who are more reactive to events and competitive initiatives.
- *Can a firm take a disciplined approach to innovation while encouraging exploration and creativity?* There should be a healthy tension between the creative side of the firm's culture and the rigor and results emphasis of the strategic activities. What is the best way to balance these left-brained and right-brained activities?
- *Can a growth laggard ever catch up to a growth leader?* This is possible, but the prospects are not encouraging. The odds of closing a growth gap improve if there is a market or technological discontinuity the growth leaders are not able to exploit.

***Looking ahead.*** This book offers actionable answers to each of these growth questions. These answers apply lessons drawn from decades of improvements in the innovation practices of organic growth leaders and strengthen them with my research into the innovation practices of hundreds of companies. The reader will find a compelling explanation of how organic growth leaders gain and sustain their growth advantages over their slower-growing rivals.

Chapter 2 explains each of the four innovation disciplines of visible leadership commitment to innovation, strategic choices of ambitious growth goals, achieved by capturing better innovation opportunities and then accomplishing the hard work of innovation. These disciplines are the energy sources for turning a growth leaders innovation flywheel faster than the rivals. Chapters 3 through 8 show how these innovation disciplines work together in a flywheel system, with a cumulative effect that is much more powerful than the sum of the parts.

The sequencing of these disciplines matters. Without a sustained commitment to innovation by a leadership team and their Board, an innovation flywheel will slow or stall. Chapter 3 shows how their investments in getting and keeping the best innovation talent gives the biggest push to an innovation flywheel. The firm's growth ambitions are shaped by the strategic choices described in Chapter 4 for finding and developing the best opportunities to innovate. How the best growth opportunities are captured and brought to market are analyzed in Chapters 5 through 7.

Growth leaders have mastered three further ingredients, to boost their innovation flywheels to turn faster. In Chapter 8, we understand why they start their innovation process from the outside in, then open this process to partners to "share to gain," and use their dashboard of innovation metrics to continuously improve their innovation processes and practices. Chapter 9 summarizes the book with answers to the five crucial growth questions.

Throughout this book we'll learn from organic growth leaders such as Adobe, Amazon, Honeywell, LEGO, Procter & Gamble, and Mastercard, about their ability to capture their opportunities sooner, while their rivals miss the same early signals of these opportunities and must eventually react to these leaders. These growth leaders attract the best innovation talent, with the mindset, skills, and capabilities to lead the intensely creative and tenacious team efforts needed to bring opportunities successfully to market.

**This book is for leadership teams** seeking to unlock the full growth potential of their firms as well as their innovation project directors and product managers, and will be valuable to thoughtful practitioners, consultants and students of corporate renewal and innovation practice. Each of these audiences will find a research-based and practice-tested approach to gaining and sustaining a growth advantage.

CHAPTER 2

# Learning from Growth Leaders

Innovation is like a tonic for boosting the organic growth rate of a firm. This pharmacological metaphor is fitting. Knowing how a drug is developed, and works is like trying to understand how firms successfully innovate. There are many active ingredients to consider, the "mechanisms of action" are hard to grasp, and the influence of each ingredient varies with the situation. The equivalent to the mechanisms of action for a drug, that work together to achieve and sustain faster organic growth of an enterprise, are these four innovation disciplines:

- Demonstrating deep leadership **commitment** to innovation with sustained investments of talent and capabilities, and by making,
- Strategic choices of **ambitious** growth goals and that are cascaded throughout the organization, to be achieved by,
- **Capturing** better opportunities sooner than rivals, and excelling with the processes of finding → screening → selecting the best concepts to develop, and by
- **Accomplishing** the work of innovation, to pursue these opportunities and achieve the firm's growth ambitions.

Each innovation discipline is a practice that an organization must master if it is to succeed. Organic growth leaders apply these four innovation disciplines through an innovation flywheel that propels them ahead of their rivals—and keeps them growing faster. When an innovation flywheel starts turning, it creates its own momentum that yields the sustained energy and resources needed for growth. Digital advances—and especially Artificial Intelligence—accelerate this flywheel by enabling faster and deeper communications and analyses. The rotational energy of an innovation flywheel is sustained by continuous learning and improvement.

## HOW INNOVATION GENERATES GROWTH

An innovation is something new that makes a difference. Something *new* could be a new product or service, a new business model or a new customer experience. It is not about new technology as such, but how advances in digital or life science technologies enable innovations. Consequential innovations emerge by combining *what's needed* by the pull of the market, and *what's possible* through the push of technological possibilities and then adroitly applying the four innovation disciplines to bring them together:

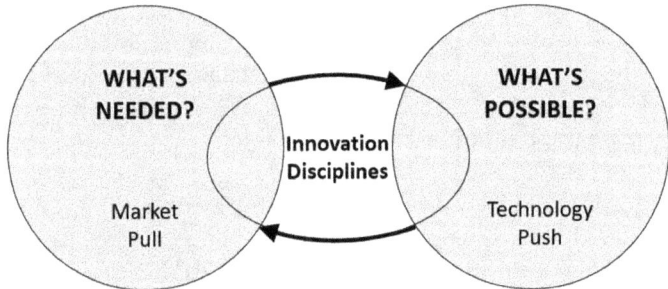

This push–pull interaction enabled the start-up MightyFly, to develop a large autonomous hybrid cargo drone. Their drone was the size of a small single-seater plane and could carry 100 pounds of cargo about 600 miles. The technology push came from advances in lightweight materials, batteries and electric engines. The market pull was from the fast-growing need for expedited deliveries from manufacturer to supplier or from a warehouse or pharmacy to remote locations such as farms or construction sites.

An unbalanced approach—that privileges either market needs or technological capabilities over the other—hurts the quest for growth. This was the conclusion of Shin Sakane, a leading Japanese innovator, on the reasons for the slow growth of Japanese companies[1] during most of the past 20 years:

> The most important factor is finding a theme to work on. Many Japanese companies manage to make steady profits, but they don't produce the new products or services that they might. Instead of finding a theme, they focus on the technologies they already have, and the value they already know how to create. I think this is one of the core reasons for their not growing.
> For example, some electronics companies – active in the electronics world, with global sales and marketing networks – have narrowed their scope to niche categories, like liquid crystal TV. They use the same core materials, and reach for the same resources, each time. It's better to look for a theme based on customer needs. What do people want that they don't have yet and that isn't available elsewhere?

The interaction of market needs and technological possibilities is reinforcing; one gives rise to the other. This is why an *invention*—the creation of something new—is different from an *innovation* using several or many inventions to change behaviors. Consider the *i*Phone; touch screens, mobile communications, user interfaces and the "home" button already existed. Yet this was a transformative innovation creating a vast ecosystem of media content, telecommunications and application development.

Invention is crucial; documenting, protecting, and leveraging inventions is the cornerstone of innovation. But it is not the only lens needed to unlock the potential of innovation. There are other perspectives on innovation we'll use to understand what sets organic growth leaders apart:

**Innovation is aspirational.** Routine, incremental improvements help a firm protect their core business but won't transform their market or apply emerging technologies to gain a new advantage. Growth leaders like Airbnb or LEGO are not incrementalists. They have bolder yet plausible aspirations for innovation that begin with ambitious objectives for organic growth that are cascaded through their organizations. Their aspirations—in the form of performance targets and timelines—are supported with abundant resources.

Growth laggards suffer the tyranny of low aspirations and confirm the truism that organizations rarely exceed modest goals. Their resources, capabilities and leadership commitment to innovation modestly match the limited goal. The organization gets the message that most sales or profit growth will come from efficiency gains and the avoidance of risk. Any innovation—such as it is—will be slow-paced and reactive.

**Innovation is disciplined.** Peter Drucker[2] viewed innovation as a skill that could be learned and practiced, like playing a musical instrument. He believed innovation was about devising a systematic way of identifying opportunities that provided new value for customers and then exploiting them with disciplined work: "*What all successful entrepreneurs I have met have in common is not a certain kind of personality, but commitment to the systematic practice of innovation.*"

Treating innovation as a discipline also dispels three misconceptions. The first is that innovation and creativity are the same. Firms thinking this way will bring their best people together for a brainstorming session to solve a problem or devise a solution. While awesome ideas are valuable, they must be implemented quickly to have impact. Too often these ad hoc groups are disbanded before there is an action plan in place. Another misconception is that innovation discipline is restrictive by not allowing for the free flow of ideas. The opposite is more accurate; discipline constrains and channels creativity and encourages better ideas. A final misconception is that innovation mostly happens within R&D. In growth-leading companies everyone at every level is motivated (and rewarded) to think about improving how the firm engages with customers, defends against competitors, and applies advances in technology.

**Innovation processes are iterative.** A wide-angle, outside-in lens takes the vantage point of present and prospective customers, collaborators, and competitors to reveal growth opportunities. This lens overcomes the narrowing effect of an inside-out approach that asks, "...how else can we deploy our resources, technologies, and capabilities to achieve our growth aspirations?" This is an essential question but when asked prematurely, it narrows the range of possibilities to what is familiar and comfortable. It is not that one approach is better on its merits, but the outcome is superior when the process starts from the outside in and iterates rapidly.[3]

**Innovation is risky.** Each type of innovation has a different degree of risk. Incremental *or small i* innovations to existing products, services, or business models are the least risky. Surprisingly, I found the probability of failure of these incremental innovations is between 25 and 40%, depending on the industry, the timing of the innovation (are you the first mover or just an imitator?), and the company's ability.[4] Too many are imitations that match a rival's innovation but lack a reason for buyers to switch. Adjacencies and **BIG I** innovations that disrupt or transform markets have probabilities of failure between 40 and 80% but promise much greater rewards to offset this higher risk.

These risks are looming especially large for meat substitute pioneers such as Beyond Meat and Impossible Foods. There is a real appetite for sustainable and animal-friendly alternatives and the enabling technology is improving both the taste and texture of plant-based hamburgers and steak. Yet vegetarians question the necessity of cell-based meat when there are plenty of plants, and high prices are a deterrent. The surge of inflation in 2022 pushed the prices of substitutes relative to meat even higher, due to the intensity of processing and rising ingredients costs. The stock market has delivered a sobering verdict by cutting valuations in the category by 94% from their peak in 2021.

Growth leaders approach the inevitable risks of innovation as learning opportunities, by reframing failures as "disappointments." Their open mindset gives them the confidence to conduct postmortems of the failures and seek ways to overcome the problems. A revealing probe I often use while facilitating a strategy session with a leadership team is "What share of your present cash flows come from innovations that emerged from an earlier failure?" Predictably, growth laggards viewed a failure as a mistake for which someone is to be blamed and can't find an answer. The same question asked of growth leaders prompts healthy introspection and the conclusion that their early failures spawned new opportunities that may be generating as much as 40–50% of their current cash flow.

**Innovation is future forward.** Innovating is like going to a party: arrive too early and there are no guests but arrive too late and you are cleaning up the trash. Capturing an opportunity takes foresight to spot it early and launch when the time is right.

Growth leaders see opportunities sooner than others and build their capabilities in advance. This gives them strategic options they can act on when the time is right. Having such options helped Sephora, the global beauty retailer, maintain their momentum during the pandemic. During the COVID-19 lockdown the company's signature blend of in-store ambience, personalized experience, and generous samples gave them no protection from strong challenges by Ulta and Amazon. But earlier observations of exercise clubs and dating sites had led Sephora's leaders to be intrigued with the idea of using a gamification model. They used market tests to confirm that adding point scoring, friendly competition, and rewards would increase customer engagement. They also experimented with engaging clients through online and mobile platforms, finding success with a Virtual Artist app that allowed clients to "try on" makeup through their phones.

Sephora's foresight gave them an edge over rivals when they had to quickly pivot toward an online world. With prior investments in augmented reality and facial recognition technology, they made beauty products an engaging game. Sephora clients could try makeup with geographically dispersed friends, experiment with new products, walk through a virtual store, and even talk to a live consultant.

**Innovation creates competitive advantages** (and overcomes disadvantages). Getting and keeping an advantage in a contested market is a never-ending task. As Andy Grove[5] famously said when he was CEO of Intel, "Success breeds complacency. Complacency breeds failure. Only the paranoid survive!" This is a useful warning when most competitive advantages are transitory, being eroded by competitive moves and changes in customer requirements, abetted by technological advances. While growth leaders have the upper hand (so long as their success doesn't breed complacency) a growth laggard can exploit turbulence and discontinuity to overcome their disadvantages.

In 2024 Apple saw the advances in Generative AI as a means to overcome their also-ran position in the smart speaker market. Their expensive, high sound resolution HomePods didn't meet the needs of most customers for affordability and connectivity. Apple's innovators envisioned an AI-powered version that could deal with requests like, "We're going away for a week. Set our devices to make sure the house is secure and doesn't use more electricity than necessary."

Will Apple's efforts be enough to overcome the advantages of Amazon's Alexa smart speaker, which dominates the market with an installed base of half a billion devices? Amazon will also see how Generative AI could give their devices fresh relevance. This predictable clash of tech titans will be echoed in every market, putting pressure on leadership teams to anticipate opportunities to capture ahead of rivals and follow through with financial backing and investments in the scarce talent that can give customers what they want.

## The Organic Growth Imperative

There are many ways to grow the top and bottom lines of a firm. These are arrayed on the spectrum from organic to inorganic growth in the boxed insert ("Which Way to Grow?"). My emphasis in this book is on the organic end of this spectrum, and how growth leaders can outpace their rivals by growing faster from within with their own resources.

Why this emphasis? Because superior organic growth signifies past competitive success while positioning a firm for success in the present and better preparing the firm to profit from an uncertain future.[6] It is the main yardstick for measuring the health of a firm and the overall competency of the leadership team. Investors want to know about future growth prospects that may propel a firm ahead of its rivals, to gauge the attractiveness of the stock price.[7] Prospective employees gravitate to growth leaders, because they promise better opportunities.

Growing faster than the market with the innovation talent and capabilities of the firm—and doing this consistently for many years—is difficult.

> **Which Way to Grow?**
> It is simplistic and counterproductive to limit the strategic choices to organic (make) or inorganic (buy). These are endpoints to a continuum of possibilities. Savvy firms use all of them to complement their organic growth initiatives perhaps by building an ecosystem of open innovation partners with scarce knowledge or capabilities. Firms in turbulent technology environments often buy small stakes in promising start-ups to for early insights into an emerging technology.

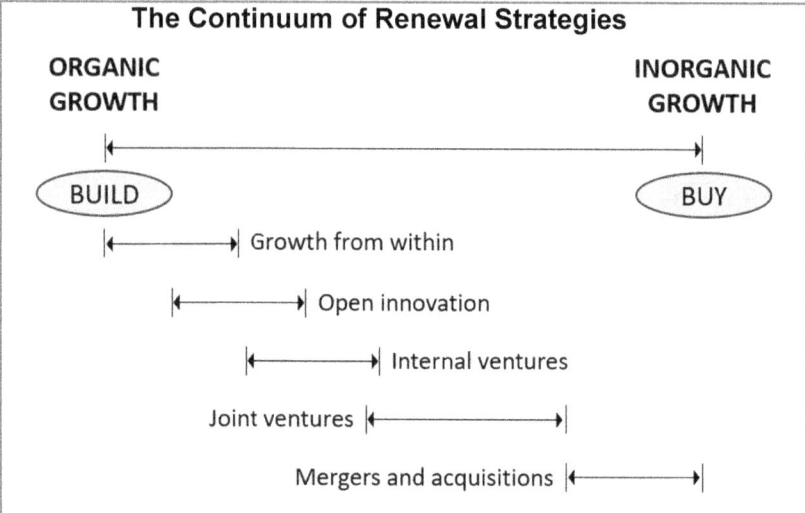

Cisco became the biggest provider of networking solutions and a pioneer in cloud computing by investing at every point along this continuum. At the "Build" end they have 25,000 engineers in project teams to improve current products or develop the next generation. These people often collaborate in open networks with ecosystem partners to access new technologies or market concepts. For emerging technologies they have an internal incubator with a direct line report to the CEO. They are also a serial acquirers of a steady stream of smaller, programmatic possibilities, often starting with a small stake in a start-up venture. If the start-up succeeds, they "spin in" the venture to obtain technology and talent.

Only 18% of the firms in my study were growth leaders that sustained a faster pace of organic growth for at least five years. Their rivals succumbed to some toxic combination of reactivity, leadership neglect, complacency, overconfidence, or short-term earnings pressures. Nokia lost their dominance in the early years of the smartphone market by focusing on short-term earnings and were reluctant to replace their aging Symbian software platform. This left Nokia unable to match the seamless customer experience of the Apple iPhone or the versatility and openness of the Android platform.[8]

Persistent growth laggards were 36% of the firms. They were hindered by an episodic commitment to innovation. When market demand was robust, they enthusiastically invested in innovation activities. When demand slowed, they cut their spending on innovation and resorted to acquisitions or cost cutting to meet their growth expectations. These expedient moves had corrosive effects on their culture and innovation capabilities and signaled to their employees and partners a weak commitment to innovation.

The remaining 46% of firms grew at about the same rate as their industry or served markets. Some of these average performers had brief spurts of above average organic growth but didn't have the innovation disciplines they needed to sustain this pace and regressed back to the mean.

*Fast growth or faster relative growth?* It is difficult for firms to grow at a fast pace for many years. A recent study of the top quartile of growing companies in 1985 found that most fell out of the top quartile over time.[9] Of these 170 original fast growers in 1985, only seven appeared in the top quartile every year for 34 years. Some of these successful growers, like Danaher and Johnson & Johnson, kept growing with large, successfully integrated acquisitions that expanded their portfolios into diverse industries.

Most fast growers (appearing in the top quartile of growth rates) eventually confront the tyranny of their slowing industry life cycle. Emergent industries and markets grow fast from a small base. Like humans these industries inevitably mature. Life cycle extensions may sustain a faster growth rate, but eventually the industry slows toward the pace of the economy.

## THE INNOVATION DISCIPLINES OF GROWTH LEADERS

Organic growth leaders share a coherent and compelling narrative about their past successes and future ability to innovate. Spend time with their people and you'll hear a refreshingly upbeat and constructive perspective on innovation: "*If you want to get ahead, build a new business...well-intentioned failures are learning opportunities...we value calculated risk-taking....*"

Within growth laggards the prevailing narrative (if there is any conversation about innovation) is usually discouraging: "*Immediate needs soak up our innovation resources... There are no carrots when it comes to innovation, only sticks... Any innovation activities are usually just added to our responsibilities.*" I heard such a self-defeating narrative while investigating why a slow-growing, alcoholic beverages firm found continued difficulty in getting their senior leaders to support innovation projects. When I interviewed these leaders, I heard a defeatist story of a company that believed their market was tired of new products, and where competitors would quickly match one another's moves. The interviews revealed an aversion to the uncertainty of innovation, and an assumption that once a new beverage was launched, it was too late to fix problems. This growth-denying narrative explained their anemic performance.

### *Changing the Narrative*

What actions will encourage a growth-affirming narrative? For answers I talked at length with 24 senior innovation leaders in global companies and then surveyed another 192 innovation leaders (See Appendix A for details about this research study) to assess 18 possible interventions, such as opening the innovation process to partners, lean thinking, starting an innovation Boot Camp, encouraging "fast-to-fail" experiments or loosening the governance structure. There was deep frustration that following all this well-meaning advice would spread scarce managerial attention over too many initiatives, confuse the organization, and complicate implementation. One leader compared this to going from symptoms to surgery without a diagnosis.

---

**Who Are the Organic Growth Leaders?**

This is not an easy question to answer. Financial statements don't reveal how top-line or earnings growth was achieved: At what point does the growth attributed to an acquisition after is has been integrated, revert to organic growth? How should growth from partnerships, joint ventures and licenses be treated? Leadership requires doing better than a reference set of competitors. Should this set be broadly or narrowly defined? In convergence industries (entertainment, communications, and computing) the competitive set is fluid and boundaries are blurring, and the relevant competitive set may be the entire ecosystem of partners.

Past organic growth leadership doesn't mean the firm will grow fast in the future. There is drag from the "incumbents curse," where past success breeds complacency and arrogance. Meanwhile, envious competitors are watching and learning, with the aim of matching the leader or even leapfrogging. Leadership commitment to the painful choices and sustained investments needed to make innovation succeed may waver under short-run earnings pressure, or a new leadership team may prefer the quicker-pay-offs from cost cutting.

We identified growth leaders by using three measures to reduce our reliance on flawed lagging measures. Past performance was based on the average annual rate of organic growth relative to competitors in the past five years. The present commitment to innovation was assessed by current spending on innovation relative to major competitors, and future prospects were based on the confidence of the management team that organic growth targets for the next three years could be achieved. With these three measures we were able to cluster firms into those who were growth leaders, average performers, and growth laggards.

My diagnosis is based on the four variables that best distinguished growth leaders (18% of firms) from growth laggards (36% of firms). These variables help define the four innovation disciplines. The four variables in order of their influence were: (1) "Invest in innovation talent," and perhaps the most important step the leadership team can take to demonstrate their strong **commitment** to innovation. (2) "Encourage prudent risk-taking." Growth leaders infuse careful risk-taking into their **ambitious growth strategies**, (3) "Adopt an outside-in innovation process" to **capture better opportunities**, (4) "Align metrics in the innovation dashboard with incentives," to help accomplish **the work of innovation**.

### *The Innovation Flywheel Effect*

These innovation disciplines work together to turn the innovation flywheel of a growth leader faster than any of their rivals.[10] Each rotation of this flywheel starts with a strong push by the first discipline of sustained leadership commitment of their scarce attention and resources toward innovation activities. Their propulsive energy is boosted by the second innovation discipline of the choice of an ambitious growth strategy, and aimed by the third discipline toward capturing the best opportunities. The final push in each rotation of the flywheel is by accomplishing the work of innovation faster than their rivals to get the chosen opportunities to market and create unstoppable momentum. This cumulative flywheel process is shown in Fig. 2.1.

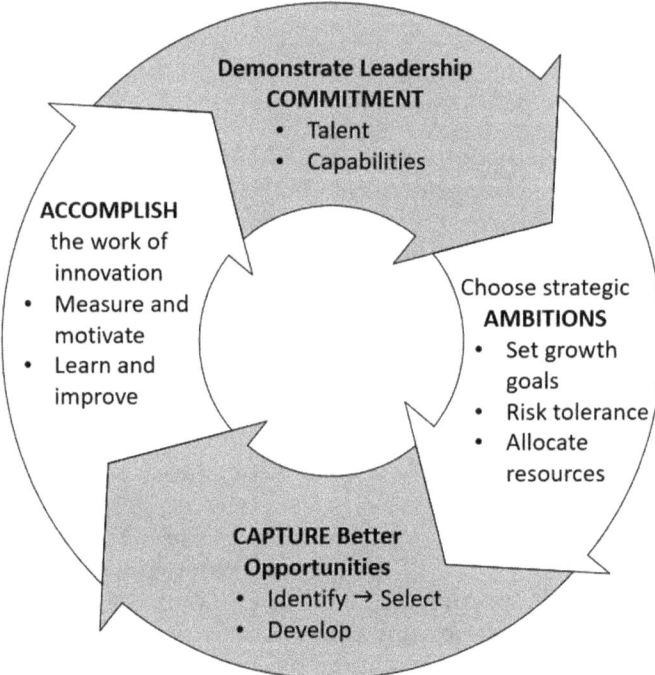

**Fig. 2.1** Turning an innovation flywheel

The effects of the four disciplines working through this flywheel are cumulative. You can't possibly identify a single big push of any innovation discipline that propelled a growth leader ahead. They work together through sustained effort, applied in a consistent direction. Some pushes may have been stronger than others, but any single push is a small fraction of the cumulative effort.

Growth leaders—from Adobe to Amazon—evolve their own versions of this innovation flywheel so it is superior to their rivals and has more cumulative momentum. Their continuous improvements came through trial-and-error experimentation and learning from best practices in other industries. Their effects are traced through their innovation dashboards; if the metrics in the dashboards don't move in the right direction the reasons are found and corrected. Growth leaders are never satisfied with their flywheels: their quest to improve keeps them ahead.

The energy that keeps an innovation flywheel spinning faster is leadership commitment reinforced by successful results. Further impetus comes from an urge to satisfy collective curiosity: "Where are the best opportunities? What can be done to improve the metrics in the dashboard? What can we learn from our partners and best practices?" Finding the answers is aided by digital technologies and especially Generative AI that unlocks insights scattered through the company.

There is a compelling logic to sustaining the momentum of this flywheel. If you aspire to grow faster, you are also committed to providing resources and finding the talent needed to capture growth opportunities before the rivals. This logic also keeps growth leaders investing steadily—in good times and bad—to sustain their momentum. Laggards and average performers are more likely to reduce their investments in the innovation disciplines when their profits come under pressure and then lose momentum. When they do decide to grow faster and catch up, it takes enormous effort to start their innovation flywheels turning again.

Starbucks sustains the momentum of their innovation flywheel, with an aspiration to deliver on their mission of "one person, one cup, and one neighborhood at a time." They signaled this commitment in 2017 by investing in digital talent and giving them the resources to offer a fully personalized customer experience. Because they can capture billions of data points each year they can obtain deep insights into every facet of the end-to-end customer experience. They do this with a cross-disciplinary team of designers, product managers, and data scientists equipped with a technology platform that is fed data from 90 million weekly transactions. This platform is augmented with data about locations, shop profiles, weather, and local events, to power personalized offers delivered via mobile phones or in the store. By the end of 2021 Starbucks was able to increase the number of offer variations by 100,000 times, while cutting the time to develop offers by 90%, and boosting their organic growth rate.

### *Turning an Innovation Flywheel Faster than Competition*

To sustain their momentum, growth leaders send successive waves of flywheel teams to capture emerging opportunities sooner and bring each to market rapidly at scale. They stay alert to the insidious organizational frictions that might slow their innovation flywheels. They are continually challenged to balance their long-run investments in organic growth and innovation against the short-term demands of the existing businesses.

Overcoming these frictions is difficult for all firms, but growth leaders know if they don't prevail, they'll surely lose ground to more nimble and motivated rivals.

Their leadership teams are attuned to these issues and ask, "OK, what should we be doing about them?" while coping with economic turbulence and keeping all their stakeholders satisfied with short-run results. They are like adventurers embarking in a caravan journey in ancient times. Their success requires the resources and will to keep going, with a strong push from the four innovation disciplines learned from earlier explorers who had successfully completed the journey. Here is how this book will apply these lessons and generate sustained and faster organic growth.

**Demonstrate leadership COMMITMENT to innovation.** This is an essential discipline to master—but not sufficient on its own—to turn an innovation flywheel faster. The best signal of leadership commitment is the collective investment of their attention to recruiting, developing, and keeping the best innovation talent. This ensures the best people are in place as implementers, project leaders, and team facilitators, to ensure the best opportunities are developed faster than the rivals. Some of their personal capabilities can be developed as the job, but the most important capabilities will have to be the basis of their assignment to the job.

To reinforce their investments in talent I found that the growth leaders were also better at developing their capabilities for doing the work of innovation. Chapter 3 describes how growth leaders cope with the inevitable uncertainties of innovation with an experimental mindset, more agile development processes and a willingness to open their processes and work with complementary collaborators. This chapter concludes with an action agenda for the leadership team and the board that demonstrates their full-throated commitment to innovation.

**Have AMBITIONS to grow faster.** A growth strategy is a credible statement of growth ambitions, risk tolerance and resource commitments. This strategy serves as a compass heading, giving direction to the search for organic growth opportunities and guiding strategic choices. Chapter 4 shows how these strategic choices close the gap between the growth goals and the momentum of the current strategy.

A growth strategy answers four questions: **Ambitions**. How fast do we want to grow relative to our rivals and industry peers? How much will come from organic growth and how much from other strategies for renewal (see the previous boxed insert "Which way to grow?"). To realize these growth ambitions the strategy should be clear about: **Allocations**..

How much are we prepared to spend to close the growth gap? What is the allocation of innovation resources to "small $i$" incremental innovations versus adjacencies or "BIG I" disruptive innovations? **Arenas.** How widely will we search for opportunities? What arenas are out-of-bounds? **Approaches.** Will we be a first mover or a fast follower? Adopt a closed, open, or hybrid approach to innovation?

While organic growth takes longer than acquisitions, it usually yields better risk-adjusted economic returns. If a firm has a solid track record of superior organic growth, equity markets will expect it to continue this pace, and reward this firm with a premium price-to-earnings ratio. At the same time, there is less debt to carry, and the organization is less stressed. As the firm builds new technology and deeper, better capabilities and gains insights into opportunities in adjacent markets, it has a more stable platform on which to continue to grow.

**CAPTURE better opportunities sooner than rivals.** Growth leaders stay ahead by better applying the third discipline of *searching* widely for potential opportunities, *evaluating* their prospects and fit with the growth strategy, and *selecting* the most promising concepts to develop. How they do this is the theme of Chapters 5 and 6.

Slower growing firms usually take a reactive approach to capturing opportunities; R&D promotes opportunities enabled by advances in the technologies they know best; distributors, salespeople and employees will suggest new services; there will be relentless pressure to match or leapfrog rivals by imitating their innovations; and changes in the business strategy will require (and inspire) supporting innovations. These sources of opportunities should always be encouraged to keep the firm in the game but won't do much to accelerate growth.

Organic growth leaders don't wait for opportunities to materialize before reacting. They start with a *wide-spectrum framework* that reimagines and stretches each dimension of their business model and customer value proposition to reveal growth possibilities. This approach can generate an overwhelming number of possibilities which they quickly reduce by applying heuristics or simple rules they have learned over time.

**Accomplish the work of innovation to ACHIEVE the Ambitions.** Organizational elephants can dance; but only when effectively mobilized and led.[11] Their innovation DNA is inhibited with an emphasis on familiar routines, myopic cultures and an absence of leadership commitment. Growth leaders overcome these inhibitors by excelling at the hard work of the fourth discipline. They encourage growth-affirming stories about surmounting barriers, celebrating success, and learning from their disappointments. Chapters 7 and 8 show how they overcome the major inhibitors to the work of innovation.

- *Risk aversion*. All leadership teams are anxious about the likelihood of success of the innovation projects in their portfolio. These uncertain prospects are paralyzing for growth laggards, while energizing for growth leaders who are more willing to share risks with partners and contain risks with frugal experimentation and lean processes.
- *Protective cultures*. As firms mature, they become more cautious. Their priority shifts to extracting maximum value from the existing resources and assets, and the time horizon shortens. Efficiency is now the emphasis and innovation activities take a back seat when the leadership team meets.
- *Diffused accountability*. This syndrome especially afflicts growth laggards who are congenitally slow to react to opportunities and get them to market. It is exacerbated by shifting priorities, episodic leadership commitment and lack of resources.
- *Misaligned metrics and incentives*. Most leadership teams lack confidence in their dashboard of innovation metrics and can't connect individual and group incentives to innovation performance. One reason is an over-reliance on long-term outcome or "tail-pipe" measures, such as the percentage of sales from products launched in the past three years. These measures are too far removed from day-to-day innovation activities to be useful motivators.

This fourth discipline is the internal system for accomplishing the work of innovation. This happens through the organizational levers that define the work to be done. Their collective action is amplified by three ingredients that give the innovation flywheel a further boost. The first ingredient starts with the pull of market needs and uses an outside-in approach. The second ingredient involves collaborating with partners and recognizing that, "not all the smart people work for us." A third ingredient completes each rotation of the innovation flywheel, by learning and improving all the subsequent turns. Growth leaders have dashboards of innovation metrics they trust and use for determining incentives, score-keeping, learning what has worked and where improvements are needed.

### *Sustaining Faster Growth*

Each innovation discipline is needed to keep a firm growing. Lack of discipline puts brakes on an innovation flywheel and slows the organic growth rate to the average for the sector. All my evidence and experience support the importance of a vigorous push from leadership commitment to propel this flywheel faster.

Episodic or limited leadership engagement and support of innovation activities is soon noticed throughout the organization. This seriously compromises the growth ambitions and the appetite for taking risk, while reducing the incentives to learn and improve. These brakes also slow the pace of innovation activities, until there is a surprise or shock from the outside the firm must respond to and overcome. A competitive disruption, the defection of a key customer, an emerging technology that was seen too late, and other unwelcome shocks may briefly tighten innovation discipline. But the need to maintain current earnings and cash flows soon compromises and slows the growth flywheel, until this precipitates another belated push on the wheel.

Growth leaders are better at balancing the protection of their core business with the pursuit of emerging opportunities. They don't view them as "either-or" choices and seek "both-and" solutions. Chapter 9 summarizes the book by answering the five crucial questions about how innovation can drive faster growth, first raised in the Introduction. Following this guidance should keep the growth leaders ahead. But if they falter—and slow their growth to an average growth rate—they open the way for their slower rivals to catch up by applying the four innovation disciplines to give a stronger push to their innovation flywheels.

**My purpose with this book** is to help leadership teams achieve and sustain superior organic growth. This is an opportune time to adopt a disciplined approach to innovation. There is mounting turbulence that creates opportunities for those who see them sooner: Customers are more demanding and technological advances are obsoleting systems, disrupting markets, blurring industry boundaries, and attracting new competitors. Firms that master the four innovation disciplines will have an advantage in navigating this turbulence and will have gained an enduring growth advantage.

CHAPTER 3

# Demonstrating Leadership Commitment to Innovation

A leadership team wants to send their organization a strong signal that innovation that generates faster organic growth is their highest priority. What could they do to push their company's innovation flywheel so forcefully that everyone gets the message: employees in all functions, board members, partners, and investors? Their strongest signal is sent through their sustained involvement in recruiting, developing, and keeping the best innovation talent. This commitment to getting and keeping the best possible innovation talent is reinforced with investments in the capabilities needed to do the work of innovation and strengthen collective foresight.

Growth leaders affirm their commitment to innovation in a way that suits their industry, company culture, and history. What works for an electronics firm or consumer goods company will be different from the asset manager BlackRock that doubled their Assets under Management (AUM) to $9.4 Trillion between 2014 and 2024. They attributed this growth to heavy investments in their end-to-end digital platform Aladdin. This platform gave BlackRock deeper knowledge to innovate with their risk analytics, by extracting opportunities from their vast data factory, and gaining deep insights into decisions about talent management.[1] This was a notable departure from industry norms that business unit heads were accountable for spotting, developing, and retaining the innovation talent.

© The Author(s), under exclusive license to Springer Nature Switzerland AG 2025
G. S. Day, *Innovate to Grow*, Palgrave Executive Essentials, https://doi.org/10.1007/978-3-031-77673-1_3

The talent policies were set by a Human Capital Committee with all 35 business heads, and only one senior HR leader. This committee had full oversight on sustaining their culture while growing fast and avoiding the silos that trap information.

## INVESTING IN INNOVATION TALENT

Innovation is a team sport requiring intensely creative and tenacious collaboration in the face of frequent setbacks, resource and time constraints, and resistance from the operating culture. But who is on the team? In my survey as I reported in Chapter 2, the single best discriminator of organic growth leadership was the commitment of the leaders to making sustained investments in innovation talent. This finding was reinforced during in-depth interviews where I heard many statements like, "We can't promote the best technical people if they don't know how to manage people and projects" and "Innovation benefits from diversity in the membership of project teams, so you can't afford to take the easy way out of assigning whoever is available." Some respondents cited the longer-term benefits from nurturing the future company leadership. One leader said, "You are not just hiring and developing innovation talent—this job is a great training ground for senior jobs."

Few firms make innovation talent a high priority. As the CMO of a multinational packaged goods company that had just missed an emerging opportunity, ruefully said, "We put our best people on our biggest brands to protect earnings, and everyone gets the message." This confirms the results from a question asking my sample of innovation leaders to rate their firms how they prioritized investments in talent:

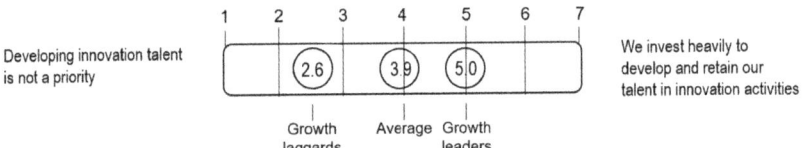

Even the growth leaders rated themselves quite low on this scale. There is a lot of space for improvement by all firms that need the strong engagement of the members of the leadership team to find the best talent, to develop their competencies and win the talent war by retaining the best innovation leaders.

***Engage the leadership team.*** Progress on the innovation talent challenge starts by the CEO making the chief human resources officer (CHRO) a strategic partner. With a resolute CHRO taking a lead role, the leadership team can address big questions such as the following:

- Are we considered an employer of choice by the people we want to hire?
- What is the retention rate for our top innovation talent, and how can we improve it?
- Are any headhunters trying to recruit our innovation talent? What does that tell us?
- How much are we investing in our "pipeline" of talent? Is there a career path for developing project leaders/team leaders?
- What are the stories about innovation successes and failures we tell around here? Do they feature the actions of individuals and teams?

Answers to these questions will help the leadership team calibrate the size of the challenge ahead of them and design an improvement program:

***Find the best talent.*** The need for talent arises when a firm wants to staff an innovation initiative or find project leaders. One approach is to assign the "best and the brightest" employees with long-term potential. This temptation should be avoided. These people are often the high potential operational leaders whose departure from their jobs would disrupt the core business. And, just because they are the best at managing the processes of the established businesses doesn't mean they are able to handle the ambiguities of an innovation project.

When assembling an innovation talent pool, look hard for people with the skills of an innovator. A study of innovative entrepreneurs[2] found they had four discovery skills: *questioning*, by asking "why?" and "what if?" that helped them to seek new possibilities. With highly tuned observing skills they could detect problems that customers experienced and learn from competitor's behaviors, to generate new ways of doing something. They were skilled at continuous *experimentation* that re-frames failures as learning experiences. By *networking* widely with counterparts in diverse settings, they discovered different perspectives and expanded their mental models. These discovery skills are all linked to an individual's latent curiosity; this was their innovation advantage.

***Select and develop innovation talent.*** Whether the innovation competencies of an individual are inherent or can be developed, was a question once tackled by a large technology company. They asked their best innovation leaders—the program managers and project directors who had championed and led several successful innovation projects—two critical incident questions: "What was your biggest success, and your greatest failure, and how did each come about?" Next, a skilled interviewer asked a series of explanatory questions to end each session by asking "What did you learn?" I've found these two questions are an excellent way to start a deep conversation with a potential candidate for an innovation leadership role. The best candidates have drawn thoughtful lessons from their successes and failures they will use or avoid in their next job.

The transcripts of these one- or two-hour dialogues were later content analyzed to find patterns in the demonstration of successful personal competencies. These competencies are arrayed along the spectrum in Fig. 3.1, from those that were "harder to develop" such as conceptual thinking and curiosity that can only be selected, to those "easier to develop" through training programs, such as technical knowledge and presentation skills.

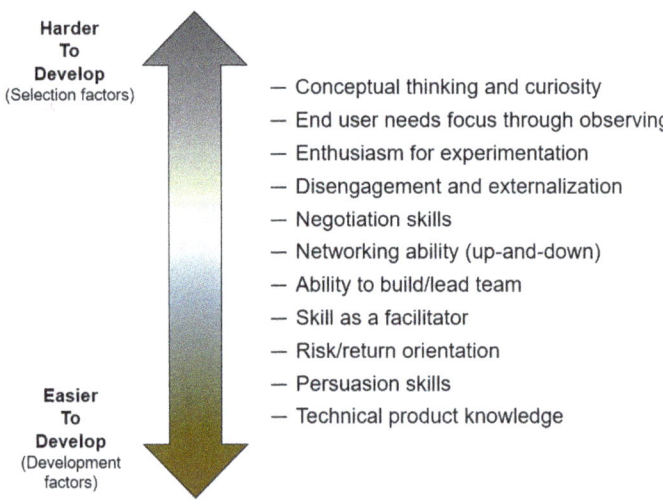

**Fig. 3.1** The personal competencies of effective innovators

This spectrum of competencies works for most firms. The "harder to develop/selection" competencies are similar to the discovery skills. The "easier to develop" competencies should be the emphasis of training programs. The CHRO should also take the lead on developing the talent with a mix of specific training to close competency gaps, reinforced by mentoring activities and job rotation programs to give an embryonic innovation leader a broad base of experience.

**Win the talent war *(by keeping the talent)*.** The scramble to find or keep the tech talent needed to apply advances in Gen AI in the past few years confirms why leadership commitment to talent distinguishes growth leaders. They saw the scarce talent they needed sooner than others and were ready. They followed through by adopting Google's[3] maxim, "Hire people that don't need support and support them."

Innovators will stay where they are valued. They won't remain in an unsupportive and uncommitted organization. Innovative talent loves innovating; they get their satisfaction from what they do best. This is what motivates them; their incentive to stay is a supportive work environment.

## INVESTING IN INNOVATION CAPABILITIES

Innovation capabilities are complex bundles of skills, technologies, and cumulative learning—exercised through innovation processes. These capabilities are not to be confused with assets such as investments in production facilities, intellectual property, or systems, because assets are things not skills. Capabilities are the glue that brings these assets together and creates economic value.

Innovation capabilities are inherently dynamic, confirming the usefulness of the distinction between *dynamic capabilities*[4] that emphasize "doing the right thing" versus *ordinary capabilities* that support the current competitive advantages by "doing the thing right." In short, effectiveness versus efficiency! Growth leaders use their ordinary capabilities to generate the cash they need to support their dynamic capabilities.

A dynamic capability is not an ad hoc solution, but a repeatable and deeply embedded set of skills and knowledge. Innovation capabilities enable firms to *sense* opportunities sooner than rivals, *seize* them better, and support the organizational *transformation* needed to stay ahead. We'll use the sensing and seizing distinction to structure this next section (as shown in Fig. 3.2) and address the transformation issues in Chapter 6.

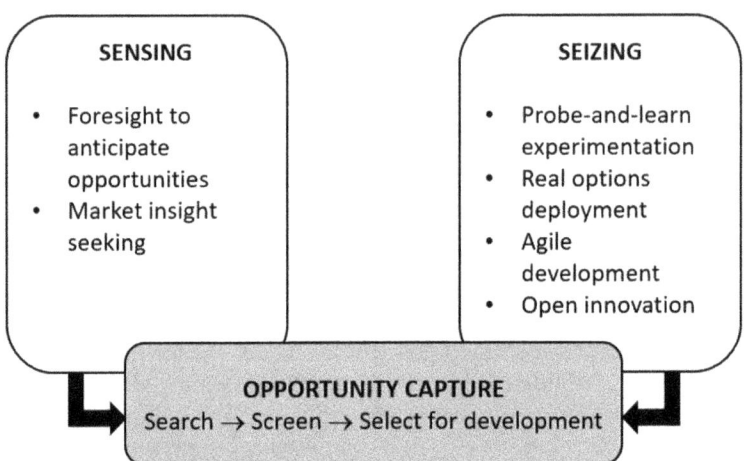

**Fig. 3.2** Innovation capabilities

Because capturing the best opportunities is so crucial to growth leadership Chapter 5 is devoted to understanding how this capability is used to push an innovation flywheel faster.

### *Innovation Sensing Capabilities*

Google was surprised when Open AI released Chat GPT in November 2022. They had less excuse for being surprised than most other firms, because they were already investing in AI through their DeepMind lab. Chat GPT triggered a "code Red" alert inside Google, and a year later they unveiled Gemini. Their version of Gen AI had an impressive ability to understand images and audio and mimic human reasoning. Google was able to train Gemini on their data and eventually gained a performance advantage in some applications.

Their inability to anticipate the introduction of Generative AI cost them a year and put them in an uncomfortable position as a laggard. Such slowness also exposed a gaping deficiency in their sensing capabilities of foresight and vigilant market insights. Growth leaders have honed these capabilities to have early visibility into what is coming over the horizon.

*Foresight to anticipate innovation opportunities.* This capability is activated through a four-stage process for scanning the periphery of a firm.

This periphery is the fuzzy zone outside the focal emphasis of the core business. This is where innovation opportunities are first detected as weak signals. The wide scope of a firm's scan of their periphery guides the subsequent activities in their foresight process:

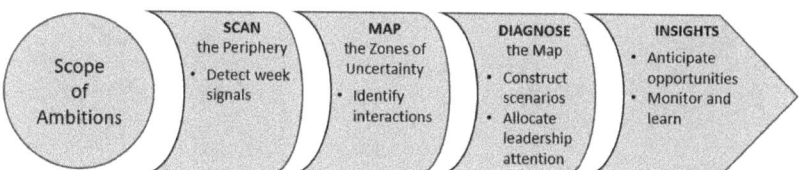

Scanning the periphery has become even more difficult because of increasing noise from irrelevant signals and an accelerating pace of change. To navigate this mounting turbulence growth leaders apply three perspectives: First, they *learn from their past* by acknowledging their past blind spots or finding an instructive analogy from precursor companies in other industries. Second, the growth leaders *approach their present* by mapping the zones of uncertainty[5] they will likely encounter in the future. The Sonoma County Wine Growers identified six of their zones and mapped them in Fig. 3.3, with the arrows between zones highlighting interactions that amplify the overall level of uncertainty.

Thirdly, growth leaders *envision new futures* with scenarios (or alternative plausible futures), to amplify weak signals of opportunities to be seized or threats to be defended against. Scenarios are usually constructed by taking the two most significant zones of uncertainty and considering the possible combinations.[6] For Sonoma Wine Growers their two biggest uncertainties were climate uncertainty and labor availability. Among their high-priority actions were finding innovations that increased carbon sequestration and reduced their greenhouse gas emissions with advances in sensor technology and data analytics.

*Insight[7] seeking.* In every market there are lurking clues about potential opportunities—if one knows where and how to look for them. This takes vigilance, aided by two ways of thinking about opportunities. One approach finds them in elusive latent market needs; these are needs that are "evident but not yet obvious." The boxed insert describes some ways to surface these latent needs. The other approach is more like detective work and extracts actionable insights from innovation disappointments.

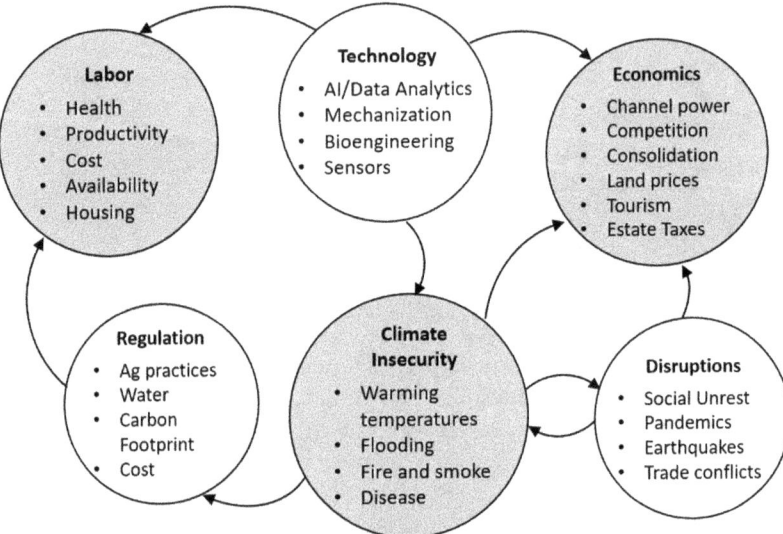

**Fig. 3.3** Zones of wine growing industry uncertainty

> **Investing into Insights About Latent Needs**
> The design thinking process[8] applies this approach to gaining insights into possible opportunities. Typically, there are four steps to this process: (1) Empathize by deeply understanding customer's problems, usually through observation, (2) Define the problem the customer is experiencing, (3) Ideate using brainstorming and other tools to generate possible solutions, and (4) Prototype and test possible concepts with users. The dominant feature of design thinking is user-centeredness which requires skilled observers who can immerse themselves in the customer's world.
>
> Many tools can be used to surface latent needs, including in-depth interviews, focus groups, problem identification, and metaphor-elicitation methods. Each requires substantial investments of time, money, and creativity. Growth laggards seldom make such investments as they are usually under pressure to deliver short-term earnings, so their opportunity horizon is shorter:
>
> To better hear the quiet voice of the customer, firms can use these approaches to learn about potential opportunities:

- Leverage lead users: These are users facing needs in advance of the rest of the market, who must find a solution to these needs.
- Diagnose complainers and defectors: Much can be learned from unhappy customers who express frustration when their changing needs are not met or understood.
- Hunt for precursors in parts of the country or the globe where fads, fashions and innovations tend to appear earlier.

Each approach has its own literature, but many interesting applications are often proprietary, especially if they are successfully extracting deeper and earlier insights.

As a litmus test of whether a firm is innovative or not, I sometimes ask how the leadership deals with failures. Growth leaders will see them as disappointments and learning opportunities. There is a supportive cultural norm within the 3M Company that avoids the word "failure" in favor of disappointment. Success and failure are not opposites; you usually must endure the second to eventually enjoy the first. Failure is sometimes a better teacher than success. The IDEO design consultancy has a slogan, "Fail often to succeed sooner." This mindset endorses taking calculated risks and learning from the results.

An "intelligent" disappointment is one that incurs a small loss but leads to learning about the reasons for the failure and possible improvements. Growth leaders create an environment of psychological safety, so failures are not hidden, and reality is fully confronted.

### *Capabilities for Seizing Innovations*

Every industry has a graveyard of innovations that failed by pursuing dead-end opportunities: Segway scooters, Quibi (short-form movies), New Coke, the Samsung Galaxy foldable phone and Google Glass each have burial plots.

All leadership teams are anxious about the prospects for their innovation initiatives—sure bets on innovation are usually trivial. But the way companies deal with this uncertainty further separates the growth leaders from the laggards. The second most influential discriminator asked about the risk posture and handling of innovation failures by the firm. This question asked about their culture, because leadership can encourage or discourage a tolerance for "well-intentioned" failures and foster a willingness to learn from them. Here are the results:

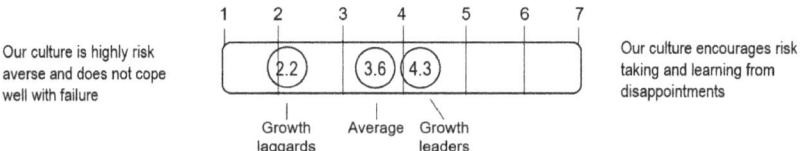

Most firms see themselves as risk averse and poor at coping with failures. They are more likely to hide a failure from view, avoid public postmortems, and seldom surface any lessons to be learned. Growth leaders are better on this measure but by their own admission they have considerable room to improve.

Learning should be emphasized throughout the development and launch process: Before a new service/business model/feature is launched and after it has fallen short in the market. Beforehand, it rarely pays to fully commit to a project before narrowing the range of uncertainty. After a disappointment the emphasis shifts to learning why the assumptions were wrong and getting insights about problems to overcome.

This advice should also apply to decisions to improve or eliminate features. When Ford got rid of their parallel parking assist feature—to save money and reduce technology bloat—the apparent reason was that their remote monitoring system revealed that few drivers were using the feature. One hopes that Ford innovators first tried to understand the reasons the feature was not being used (was it too slow? too hard to find?) and then field-tested possible improvements.

Growth leaders are better at balancing the risks and rewards of innovation. They cope with inherent uncertainty in three ways: First, they approach innovation activities with an experimental mindset and apply real options analysis to prospective opportunities, to learn about the upsides (and downsides) before fully committing. Second, they are more agile during their development processes, and can pivot faster in response to unforeseen changes in the market. Third, growth leaders are more open to sharing their gains with capable partners and collaborating with them when they bring superior capabilities. These three advantages help them capture better opportunities ahead of their rivals and each gives them a capability advantage:

*Probe-and-learn experimentation.* Small, fast experiments with quickly created prototypes or concept statements make a virtue of failing fast, by emphasizing learning.[9] Within Amazon they are likened to planting seeds or "going down blind alleys." To fully use what is learned, an organization must be willing to challenge their beliefs and assumptions about an opportunity. A probe-and-learn-mindset could have avoided a lot of grief for Zillow Group's home buying concept called "Offers." Zillow is a successful real-estate marketplace company that helps prospective home buyers answer the questions, "What is that house worth? What should we offer for it?"

In 2018 Zillow announced they would begin buying and selling homes[10] in partnership with local brokerages and agents, with the profits coming from "flipping" these homes. They optimistically projected transaction volumes of 5000 homes per month and potential revenue of $20 Billion within five years. The results fell very far short. The business was sold at a loss of perhaps $420 million three years after launch. Would a more experimental approach have avoided this loss?

The business model for "Zillow Offers" relied on their ability to forecast the future price of a home, once it was fixed up. This assumption became problematic because their forecasting algorithm often led them to pay too much for a property. Instead, they should have run small, fast experiments in diverse home markets to test how closely their algorithm estimated the appraised value. They could also have tried out their model on 10–15 homes to appreciate better the many pitfalls of flipping.

Rather than take a cautious, "learn-before-committing" approach, Zillow bought hundreds of homes in 2019 just before the pandemic distorted the market for homes. The pandemic created a surge of unforeseen demand their business model could not handle. To add to the drama the CEO was publicly and vociferously committed to the flipping strategy. In his words, it was, "go big or go home." A more cautious experimental approach to learning deeply about the risks and rewards was not on his agenda.

*Real option analysis.* This is a force multiplier when used in tandem with a probe-and-learn capability. A "real" option is a small financial bet that preserves the right to make further moves but is not an obligation. A firm might buy a real option to better understand an emerging technology or an innovation opportunity with research in its lab or make a small investment in a start-up. By being on the inside of a start-up as an investor—perhaps as a member of the board—they will become an insider and be privy to the latest information. Medtronic has made a series of investments in biotech start-ups to learn about using their technologies to improve the performance of their stents. They did not exercise their opportunity to invest more; they had learned what they needed to learn.

Growth leaders will assemble a portfolio of real options of different kinds,[11] depending on their growth goals and the uncertainties in their technology and market space:

- Preserve and protect options. These are useful when the market and technology spaces are familiar, and uncertainty is manageable. They allow a firm to respond to possible competitive moves, shifts in market requirements, or surprises in the economic climate. Such options are created through anticipatory development programs that ensure the firm isn't left behind when rivals move.
- Exploratory options. These are designed to cope with high market and technical uncertainty, before commercial feasibility has been established. These are small, exploratory investments to help a firm obtain additional experience that can later be parlayed into larger strategic commitments. Small R&D investments, joint ventures, or investments in start-ups serve this purpose.
- Scouting options are cautious investments made to discover new technologies or markets when uncertainty is quite high. The military scouting metaphor is apt: to find an enemy, the army sends out scouts—and should they fail to return, the leadership has gained some knowledge of the situation they face.

*Agile development processes.* Agility is the ability of a firm to respond rapidly to changes in their opportunity environment.[12] Changing direction quickly is especially needed when there is high uncertainty about **BIG-I** innovation opportunities Without agility a developer is left to react to the moves of others. A persistent reactor will lose most of their degrees of freedom of action and eventually will become a growth laggard.

Most firms use some form of a phase-gate or stage-gate development process to bring their innovation concepts to market. This process breaks the development process into a natural sequence of steps needed to move an opportunity concept to testing and launch. Each stage has a go/no-go decision point, where leadership must decide whether to proceed to the next stage. There is attrition in the number of projects as each stage becomes another filter. This enables "pay-as-you-go" project funding, with resources available for the next step only when there is some progress against project metrics such as the development budget, prototype performance, and cost-to-build. This stage-gate process has a deceptively tidy, linear, and sequential appearance, as befits its origin in NASA engineering projects. This process is iterative, halting, messy, and uncertain—especially for **BIG-I** projects.

Growth leaders have evolved their development processes beyond the rigid stage-gates to cope with uncertainty. Instead of a one-size-fits-all sequence, there will be heavyweight and lightweight versions appropriate for small-*i*, adjacency, and BIG-*I* projects. These variations in the development process account for the greater uncertainties of adjacencies and BIG-*I* innovations. An "efficient" standard approach to each gate (appropriate for *small-i* projects) sets early targets, under the assumption that any learning during later stages will reinforce the early stages. This process is not suited to the development of a BIG-*I* Innovation projects. As they proceed there will be surprises (both fortuitous and calamitous), and underlying assumptions will need to be revised.

Further gains in speed and productivity may come by moving to "leaner" gates. Instead of the lengthy and time-consuming preparation of gate deliverables by the innovation team, a brief document with a few backup slides is all that is needed. Gatekeepers arrive at the review meeting already knowing the project and are simply informed at the gate review about the risks and further commitments that need to be made. Standardized checklists are eliminated, and authority for deciding which activities are needed to demonstrate viability at each stage is delegated to the project teams. Firms with leaner, more agile processes can also apply advances in Generative AI to extend their advantages.

The ability of Gen AI to create novel outputs, rather than simply recognizing and finding patterns in existing data, is a potential game-changer for firms able to apply these advances to developing new concepts. There are benefits at every stage of the development process: (1) creating novel and realistic visualizations of concepts to accelerate the early stages, and obtain resources and approvals faster, (2) optimizing a chosen concept for cost, performance, and manufacturability, (3) accelerating the creation of a digital prototype for testing, and (4) speeding the evaluation of prototypes varied "what if" scenarios, and being able to compare different versions. We'll elaborate on these benefits more fully in Chapter 7.

Further gains will come from learning models built on a Gen AI platform that can be widely used throughout the firm. Fully exploiting these possibilities will be limited only by the imagination and ability of firm's innovation talent. Thus, we have come full circle to the sustainable advantages that growth leaders gain by getting and keeping the best innovation talent with the experience and know-how to use these new capabilities.

***Amplifying capabilities with open innovation.***[13] The term "open" is rich with positive connotations of flexibility, while sharing and accessing the skills and capabilities of other firms. Open innovation has been aided by advances in digital technologies for coordinating complementary partners, including design agencies and specialized suppliers of technology. The shift from closed, in-house R&D and innovation activities has been boosted by the realization that, "not all the smart people in our industry work for us," and the emergence of innovation brokers that help firms search for ideas and connect their inventors to markets.

Growth leaders such as Haier, the Chinese home appliance and electronics firm, were quick to embrace open innovation. Among their partnership platforms is one that is connected to over a million scientists and engineers through an online portal with tools for turning concepts into products. Some of their concepts emerge from their exercise of curiosity, for example about why customers were breaking their washing machines. They found many of these customers were using their machines to wash potatoes.

When an open innovation network is controlled by a firm such as Haier, the network functions like a private club. The focal firm pursues an opportunity with one or more partners with the requisite skills and experience and without unmanageable conflicts of interest. An open structure is well suited to complex solutions for solving customers' problems. For example, Janssen (Pharmaceuticals) helps doctors overcome the problem of schizophrenia patients missing their injections of medication (an issue for about 30% of these patients at any given time). Working with payers, doctors, nurses, schedulers, clinics, and a host of implementation partners, Janssen manages all the steps in the distribution of a drug to an injection site, to overcome the barriers for patients.

Open innovation is not a panacea, nor is it risk free. There is sure to be some risk from the dependence on others to innovate in tandem, and adoption-chain risk which is the extent to which the partners need to incorporate your progress before customers can assess the completed innovation. Growth leaders are less susceptible to these risks because they have robust internal mechanisms for finding competent partners and persuading them to collaborate, while keeping their supporting activities coordinated and monitoring the performance of partners to correct any potential problems before they compromise a project. These risks are worth bearing, to realize the gains in agility and overcome the inherent caution of a closed, inward-looking development process.

## SIGNALING LEADERSHIP COMMITMENT TO INNOVATION

When a leadership team makes visible investments in talent and innovation capabilities, they give their innovation flywheel a strong push. To keep it turning faster they must signal to their entire organization that innovation is a high priority. Their best signals will reinforce each other, as a "ball-of-yarn" schematic highlights. On the circumference are influential actions the Board or the leadership team—or both together—could take (Fig. 3.4).

**Talent scouting and recruiting.** To emphasize their investments in talent, each member of the leadership team should be constantly scanning for—and connecting with—prospective candidates to hire or as sources of ideas. They should be engaging with social media sites like LinkedIn, and well-connected recruiting firms, with a long-range plan to approach the best candidates. Some firms have a war room where they keep all their information about high potential innovation talent.

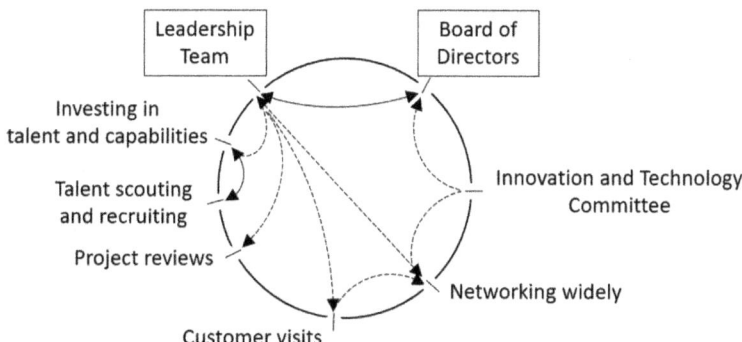

**Fig. 3.4** Signaling commitment to innovation

**Participate actively in project reviews and capability assessments.** There is perhaps no stronger signal than an informed involvement of leadership in the updates and reviews of major innovation projects. This is not a fleeting encounter but an enthusiastic and informed participation at every stage of development. Those engaged leaders can encourage small bets and experiments by making investment commitments on-the-spot, so the project stays on schedule.

**Networking widely.** Leaders need to leave the safety of their offices and anticipate how the future might unfold. As William Gibson[14] famously observed, "The future has already arrived. It's just not evenly distributed yet." Each leader should participate in cross-industry forums (and avoid industry echo chambers), visit technology pacesetters such as Microsoft, Amazon, Biogen, and venture accelerators, and participate in futures studies.

**Visiting customers, partners, and collaborators** to listen and learn about their emerging needs and current pain points. A variant I suggest to my long-time clients (because it requires shared trust) is to have each member of the leadership team visit a once-loyal customer that has apparently defected to a rival or has cut back sharply on their purchases. The aggrieved customer is usually pleased to see a C-Suite representative of the firm. They also want to explain why they defected, and what innovations and changes are needed to get the firm back into the consideration set.

**Forming a special committee** of the board of directors, to focus on innovation progress and advances in technology such as Gen AI. This has an especially high impact when visibly supported by the CEO, Chairman, and the directors. Their endorsement of innovation and organic growth then becomes embedded in the governance and resource allocation decisions.[15] A further benefit is the value of having Board members with relevant technology experience and skills, to bring informed diversity to Board meetings.

The message of this chapter is that the visible commitments of the leadership team to innovation talent and capability development are woven into the history and culture of organic growth leaders. These commitments demonstrate to the organization that innovation is a sustained priority.

CHAPTER 4

# Strategies for Achieving Growth Ambitions

A growth strategy is a declaration of a firm's growth ambitions and how they will be achieved. It is not a detailed map but gives a compass heading for navigating technology and market uncertainty with confidence. A growth strategy[1] guides the choices of opportunities and capabilities to emphasize, matches the need for resources to what is available, and motivates the entire organization with a vision of future success.

A *good* growth strategy faces reality and respects constraints, while capitalizing on the momentum from past performance. What is possible for a price-value oriented retailer such as Walmart, will be different from a cutting-edge technology firm such as Novo Nordisk or Adobe. Importantly, a good strategy faces up to the challenges and opportunities for the firm and indicates how they will be overcome.

A *deficient* growth strategy starts with timid aspirations and uncertain commitments and is afflicted by risk aversion. These problems hobble growth laggards, who suffer the tyranny of low expectations and growth-denying narratives about innovation. Their strategies try to accommodate too many conflicting demands and interests and avoid making choices. An unfortunate example is Activator Corp (disguised), a firm making aircraft systems. There were too many projects to absorb with their limited resources and few projects were finished. Instead of proper product releases, the firm had "product escapes" that were pushed out the door without adequate sales training, documentation, or support. This

© The Author(s), under exclusive license to Springer Nature Switzerland AG 2025
G. S. Day, *Innovate to Grow*, Palgrave Executive Essentials, https://doi.org/10.1007/978-3-031-77673-1_4

caused many problems; their growth faltered, and the organization was frustrated.

Activator Corp had haphazardly entered many new markets, while shifting their core technology from hydraulic systems to linear drives and confronted unfamiliar competitors. Like many growth laggards they wanted to grow faster but lacked strategic discipline. An increased investment in R&D only made their situation worse. They lacked the talent to put the resources to work and the lack of results frustrated everyone.

A good *growth strategy* answers four questions: (1) How fast do we want to grow? What portion will come from organic growth? (2) What resources will the firm's leaders allocate to organic growth initiatives? How much should be provided to initiatives beyond protecting the core business? (3) Which market arenas are attractive prospects? Which are beyond our limits? (4) How will we innovate? How much will we rely on an ecosystem of partners? The answers to these questions are interdependent; change one answer and the others must change to stay aligned.

Each part of a growth strategy is a result of tough decisions about an uncertain future. Most executives struggle with these decisions and underestimate the time and cost to make them.[2] Few firms have a disciplined way of analyzing their innovation portfolios or making decisions to delay, accelerate or kill growth projects. Some projects will be understaffed, while others are on life support. This chapter provides a disciplined approach for arriving at an ambitious growth strategy that will guide a firm toward faster growth.

---

**The Benefits of a Growth Strategy**

My research confirms the benefits of having a growth strategy to spell out how a firm can achieve its ambitions. Two questions I asked of my sample of senior innovation executives reveal why strategy matters:

- "Our process for setting a growth strategy is ad hoc and reactive":
  - Answer: 35% of laggards agreed vs 10% of growth leaders

- "If you asked people involved with innovation activities in your organization, would they say the biggest challenge is":
  - A. To get the resources, approvals, and authority needed to develop the innovation? or

> B. To actually execute the innovation task and bring the new idea to market?
>
> The second question reveals whether a firm has strategic discipline. Among growth leaders, 69% picked "execution" issues, versus the growth laggards who choose "execution" 46% of the time. Difficulties getting permission to proceed with a project are a symptom of strategic incoherence; signaling that most decisions about innovation projects are ad hoc and reactive.

There should be no ambiguity about the firm's ambitions as expressed in their growth goals, or the allocation of resources that supports these growth goals and enables their achievement. The choices of arenas and approaches are made more opportunistically as the firm tries different ways of reaching their ambitions. The primacy of Ambitions in shaping a growth strategy is highlighted in Fig. 4.1.

**Fig. 4.1** Elements of an organic growth strategy

## Setting the Growth Goals

Goals for future growth in revenue and operating profit emerge from an arduous negotiation of the divergent interests and conflicting opinions of many stakeholders. The leadership team begins the negotiations from the top-down, with ambitious targets that may satisfy their Board or the shareholders by boosting the stock price. These goals then confront a risk-averse portfolio of growth initiatives that won't achieve the desired growth. The portfolios of laggards are especially self-defeating, being mostly either improvements of the current offerings or reactions to actions by competitors.

An approach I've used with dozens of firms for negotiating realistic growth objectives has three stages: The first stage is grounded in a deep understanding of the sources of past growth. Second, is a forecast of the momentum of the present strategy, making realistic assumptions about changes in the next 3–5 years. The third stage is closing the gap between the initial top-down objectives and the likely momentum of the current strategy. This is an arduous process involving the leadership team arriving at a deep understanding of the role of innovation in filling the growth gap. Their shared journey toward a realistic growth goal is about learning, discovery, and agility.

### *Sources of Past Growth*

The recent past of a firm is the departure point for projecting the future growth prospects. To visualize how past organic growth has been achieved, start by decomposing[3] the sources of organic growth in the past year. This analysis starts by categorizing past growth gains in order to understand their sources. Management teams should avoid being caught using an inside-out frame when analyzing past growth, by using product accounting categories rather than customers. A better approach is to analyze past growth in terms of six customer-oriented categories. Figure 4.2 is an example. Four of the six sources of past growth came from the core business:

- Sales from growing the market, assuming a constant market share,
- Gains (or losses) from price changes,
- Reducing churn or defections, and
- Market share changes.

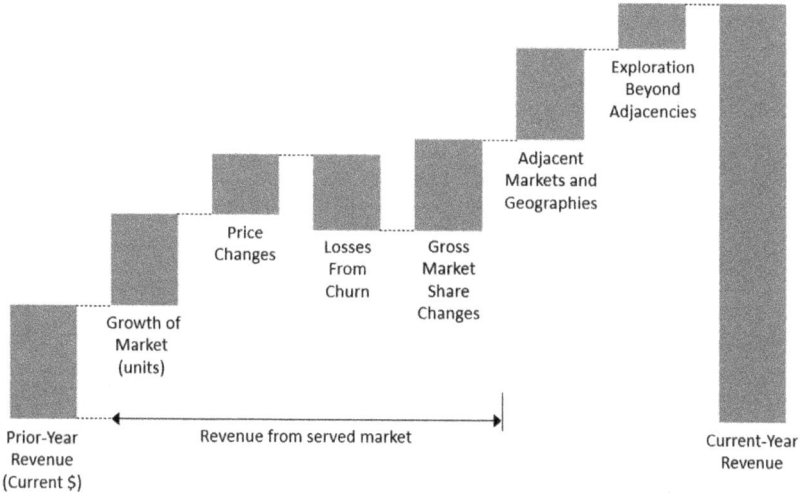

**Fig. 4.2** Past sources of organic growth* (*Excludes the effects of acquisitions)

The losses from churn or customer defections can be significant. Consider that the average firm has a churn rate of 18% per year. Reducing this churn by 2% produces a gain of 2% in the top line. Past growth may also have come from expansion into adjacent markets or geographies, and bolder initiatives to expand into brand-new product areas, geographies, or business models.

### *Forecasting the Momentum of the Current Strategy*

This projection answers the difficult question, "What will your sales and profits be in the next two, three, and five years if you *continue with your current strategy*, while adapting to anticipated changes in the market?" This is the momentum or impetus from the firm's forward motion. Will performance keep improving, or decline with the future market? Will you gain or lose market share with your current strategy? Will your prices (in real terms) decline or increase? Will there be productivity gains?

Momentum forecasting seems straight-forward—but it's not. The leadership team has to solidify their hazy assumptions about changes coming over the horizon, and then arrive at a consensus forecast. When there is a lot of turbulence there may be as many different assumptions about the future as there are members of the leadership team. By sharing and debating their assumptions the outcome will be a more coherent strategy. This is valuable when an emerging technology such as Gen AI arrives on the scene. What will be the impact on the momentum forecast? The head of HR sees benefits for sourcing talent, the Chief Commercial Officer worries about new competitors, and the CEO is energized by the prospect of a searchable database of all past projects and reports. These differences in perspective coalesce when every member of the team focuses on the impact on the firm's momentum.

Momentum forecasting is conjectural, the further into the future the greater the uncertainty. One way to deal with uncertainty is to forecast the "best-case" and "worst case" scenarios to create a cone of uncertainty.[4] The further into the future one peers the wider the cone of uncertainty. This is a healthy recognition that there are many forces to anticipate, monitor and manage.

Forecasting momentum in volatile markets is especially fraught. An instructive example is the direct-to-consumer mattress maker, Casper Sleep, that was launched in 2014. Their disruptive concept was "a mattress in a box," made with a technology that compressed a mattress enough to fit in a small shipping box. The customer unboxed it and waited a few hours for their new mattress to take shape. To reduce buyer risk, Casper let buyers keep a mattress for 100 hours and still return it.

Their business soon took off, and in 2019 Casper became a Unicorn with a billion-dollar valuation. They opened retail stores and proclaimed they would "reinvent the future of sleep." By 2020 their reported revenues were $497 million, but they still lost money. Imagine forecasting the momentum of Casper revenue for the three years beyond 2020 when they were facing 175 competing, mattress-in-a-box imitators. This included some established mattress makers who wanted to sell directly to their consumers and leverage their strong brands. With competition everywhere, the costs of acquiring new customers squeezed Casper's margins and limited their investments in innovation and international expansion. Would they have behaved differently had they made reasonable assumptions about their market, their share, and the trajectory of prices?

A useful aphorism, attributed to Niels Bohr, one of the fathers of the atom bomb is, "It is difficult to make predictions, especially about the future." When arriving at a momentum forecast this problem is compounded by spreadsheets that encourage, "the quantification of fantasy." A spreadsheet reduces messy uncertainties to overly precise linear projections that discourage creative thinking about a non-linear and uncertain future.

*Closing a Growth Gap*

The size of a growth gap is revealed through a lengthy, iterative process beginning with the leadership setting their preliminary growth goal. This goal considers three factors: (1) *Equity market expectations*. These initial ambitious for growth are advocated by senior leaders or directors aiming to boost the stock price, (2) the *ambitions* of key people who expect that increasing the value of stock options will attract talent and generate excitement in the organization, and (3) the *constraints* of the *financial capacity* of the firm to fund growth, that depend on the health of the balance sheet, the dividend policy and the borrowing capacity of the company.[5]

The initial top-down growth goal usually exceeds the momentum forecast, leaving a growth gap shown in Fig. 4.3. This gap can be closed by bending the momentum curve upward (see the boxed insert), partially filling the gap with acquisition candidates already in the pipeline (and allowing time for them to contribute), and increasing the organization's capacity to grow organically through innovation. If these moves don't move the growth dial enough, then the objectives must be negotiated downwards, or trade-offs are made in the objectives. It may be possible to reach the revenue growth goal, but not the earnings goal—or vice versa.

> **Bending a Momentum Curve[6]**
> Momentum is not inevitable; it is the forward impetus from continuing the current strategy while maintaining the beliefs, behaviors, and actions preventing a strategy from reaching its full potential. Overcoming these constraints starts with the reasons customers either don't buy (despite a superior value proposition) or defect to other suppliers. Some years ago, I found that (on average) about 18% of once-loyal customers defected to competitors each year. These defections may be hard to detect. Some customers only cut back their purchases if they have found another supplier. Others may loudly eject a supplier from their consideration set in frustration. Retaining some of these defectors would boost the organic

> growth rate accordingly. Finding this valuable source of growth starts by deeply understanding every step of the customer journey to learn the drivers and barriers, and then shaping how each customer segment traverses their journey. Deep insights into customer behavior are gained when the data are structured to be unlocked by Gen AI. It is often easier and less expensive to influence up-stream customer behavior, like calling a dealer or going to a multi-brand store, than trying to change their mind at the point of purchase.

## Allocating Resources Across the Innovation Portfolio

Aspiring to grow faster means taking bigger risks and allocating more resources to innovation. Where and how that happens depends on why there is a growth gap. Was the forecast growth gap due to a deficient pipeline of innovation projects? An adverse shift in the enabling technology? Or something else? This should trigger collective curiosity among the leadership team to find explanations.

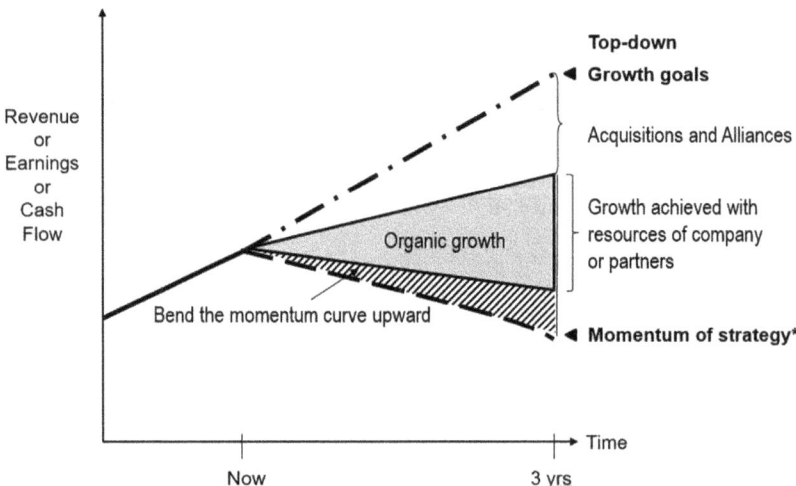

**Fig. 4.3** Closing the growth gap

By 2008 Adobe foresaw slowing growth[7] for their image-editing Photoshop software, that had earned the rare status of a product that was also a verb like Xerox or Google. Photoshop was sold as boxed software stored on a disc, giving users a perpetual license to use their software. The dominance of Photoshop was being threatened by the emergence of low-cost cloud storage. Potential rivals including Google, Microsoft, and IBM might use this technological disruption to enter their market. To counter the anticipated slowing of the momentum of their current strategy, Adobe made a pre-emptive move to the cloud with an innovative subscription model where they rented rather than sold their technology. The announcement of this move was met with outrage from loyal users who feared the storage of their creative content in an amorphous cloud. Once these users were reassured, by learning about potential the benefits to their practice, they were joined by new creators attracted by the ease of access. Fast forward from 2010, when Adobe sales were $4.4 billion, to 2024 when sales had jumped by a factor of four.

**How to diagnose an innovation portfolio.** Start by deciding where each of the current innovation initiatives falls on the continuum of risk and reward, from small-$i$ to **BIG-I** in Fig. 4.4.[8] It may be difficult to compile all the initiatives that are under way. R&D will know about the technology and new product development projects. Many of the other growth-creating initiatives may be spread through the organization: Marketing may be exploring a new end-use market with a joint venture partner, while senior management may be investing in early-stage start-ups, or considering a dramatic business model innovation.

The next step is to plot the innovation initiatives onto an innovation risk matrix that has two dimensions. One is how familiar the company is with the intended market, and the other is the similarity of the initiative to the current product or technology. This portrayal of a portfolio[9] shows the probability of failure—a proxy for the risk of each category along the innovation continuum,[10] as shown in Fig. 4.5.

Positioning a particular initiative in this matrix requires deep insight. When McDonald's attempted to offer pizza, for example, they assumed their new offering would be reasonably close to their existing fast-food items, and would appeal to their usual customers. Using that assumption, pizza would be a familiar product for the present market and would appear in the bottom left of the innovation risk matrix. But the project failed, and their postmortem showed that the launch was fraught with risk from the beginning. No one could figure out how to make or serve

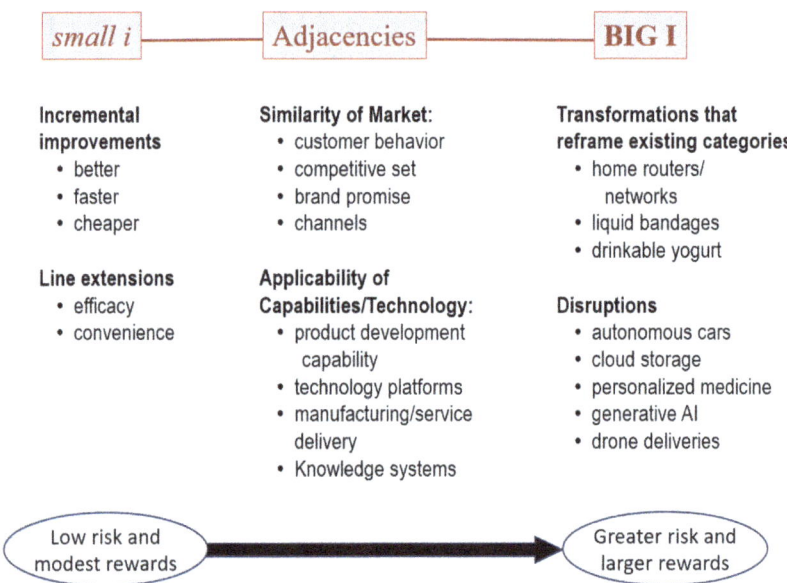

**Fig. 4.4** The innovation continuum

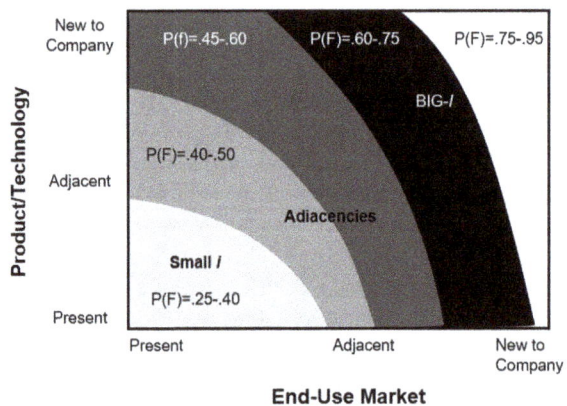

P(F) = Probability of Failure

**Fig. 4.5** The innovation risk matrix

a pizza in 30 seconds or less, and orders caused long backups at the takeout window, compromising the McDonald's service-delivery model. Their postmortem also found that the brand experience didn't give them "permission" to offer pizza.

The assessment of the portfolio should be done by a taskforce of senior managers with strategic oversight and authority over development budgets and allocations. Team members will rate each project independently and then explain their rationale. Reasons for any differences of opinion need to be understood and resolved. The balance of the portfolio is revealed by a plot of all initiatives on the risk matrix. Most will be small *i* initiatives that rarely generate much growth but stabilize and defend the core business with incremental improvements that will match or preempt the competitors. To be avoided is a portfolio with an internal traffic jam of "safe" projects absorbing the R&D resources and slowing the organization's pursuit of more ambitious initiatives with long-term impact.

The final step is forecasting the risk-adjusted revenues and profits likely to be realized from each of the initiatives in the innovation portfolio. Their contribution to closing the growth gap depends on (a) how likely they are to be developed, (b) when they are likely to be launched, and (c) their probability of success when they enter the market. Their probable contributions are then cumulated across the portfolio for each year of the planning horizon. The larger the growth gap, the less likely the current innovation portfolio is able to close the growth gap.

## *Different Ambitions, Different Allocations*

A sure way to thwart an ambitious growth strategy is not allocating enough resources to closing the growth gap. It takes time to find and capture the best opportunities and develop and launch them so they can generate revenue and cash. Another way to miss an ambitious growth objective is to avoid risk and emphasize *small-i* innovations that protect the core. These defensive moves are necessary, but usually soak up the resources that could be used to nurture longer-term growth investments.

Growth leaders vigorously defend their core, while placing bigger bets on adjacencies and **BIG-I** innovations. The study of the allocations of growth leaders[11] in different industries in Fig. 4.6 is a useful input to the inevitable debate about whether the current allocation will deliver an ambitious growth goal.

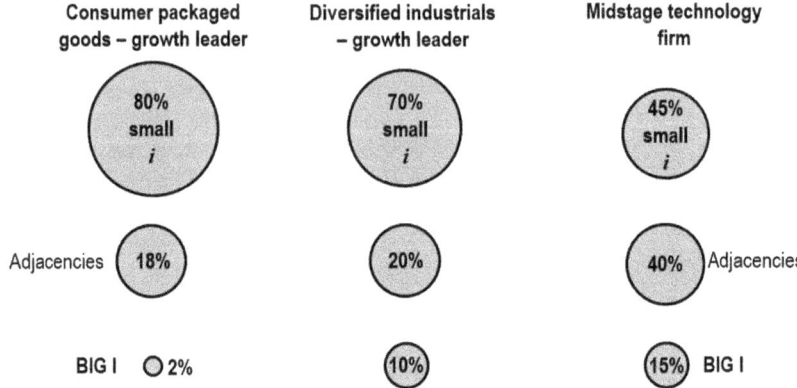

**Fig. 4.6** Different allocations for different aspirations (*Source* Nagji and Tuff [2012])

Increasing the funding of riskier longer-term innovation projects often triggers a debate over the sources of funding. Each business unit can and should fund their *small-i* projects but will resist and resent a corporate innovation tax because they won't see the benefits from distant and uncertain growth projects. A better approach is for this funding to come from a corporate innovation fund.

## Choosing Arenas and Approaches

When there is a consensus about the ambition of the goals and how resources are to be allocated, the growth strategy needs to answer two more questions:

1. What are the limits to the scope of the strategy? What arenas are out-of-bounds because they are beyond the capability of our firm?
2. How far will we open our innovation processes?

Answers to these questions won't come by imitating another firm's successful strategy. A growth strategy must be tailored to the capabilities and culture of the firm, the future prospects for the market, and anticipate advances in enabling technologies.

## Setting Boundaries and Limits

The legendary LEGO Group is a cautionary tale about the pitfalls of stretching the search for growth beyond the capabilities of the firm. In the late nineties the Danish company launched forays into video games, theme parks, and learning centers, in search of new play experiences they could provide.[12] Most of their growth initiatives lost money, and by 2003 the LEGO Group was close to bankruptcy. The company abandoned these distractions to focus on the traditional play experience and created an Enterprise platform to digitize all their key management processes.

It is tempting to look for growth in far-flung markets by finding adjacent opportunities or seeking the "blue oceans" of emerging markets. Experience teaches that these moves are more likely to be distractions that dilute financial resources or outpace the capabilities of a firm to manage the initiative and gain access to the market. This is why the risk of failure from BIG I growth initiatives is so high, and why they require careful exploration before proceeding.

Clearly specifying the scope also determines how widely the leadership team will look for early signals from the periphery of the firm. The scope should be as broad as needed to see what is changing, without wasting time and energy. Reactive firms generally focus too narrowly, as once happened to a major pet-food maker that relied on available market data that suggested the firm was keeping its dominant share in a flat market. This seemed to be good news. However, the company was losing share in a broader total market that was growing rapidly. The emergence of scientific pet-food formulas sold through nontraditional specialty outlets and veterinarians was not reflected in the company's data. While managers were vaguely aware of this trend, they were looking too narrowly at their market reports to realize they were losing ground. When they eventually realized how blinkered their scope was, they became a late and lackluster entrant in an already crowded space.

Defining scope has less to do with knowledge than collective curiosity. It hinges less on knowing the answers than posing the right questions to reveal the limits of existing knowledge, and then discovering where to look for answers. Fortunately advances in large language Gen AI models will enable deeper, faster interrogations of digital data.

Ironically, constraints also encourage creativity. Without constraints to guide innovation efforts complacency may set in, and teams may settle for any intuitively plausible idea that quickly comes to mind rather than taking time to develop alternatives that may lead to better ideas. Constraints overcome this pernicious tendency by giving focus and a challenge to people to search widely for information and connect different sources to generate richer concepts.

## *Opening the Innovation Process*[13]

Few firms have completely open innovation processes that rely on partners for key activities or restrict themselves to fully closed processes where everything is done within the organization. The closed or vertically integrated model has lost favor as firms that open their innovation processes have scored impressive gains in the quality of their ideas, faster access to technology, and time to market. A further impetus to opening comes from the recognition that many significant innovations emerge from small and medium-size firms willing to license or sell their intellectual property.

The choice to be open is not simply a matter of adding a few R&D partners, taking stakes in early-stage companies, or posting a prize on the Internet. Open innovation requires a change in mindset while giving up some ownership control. The shift from closed to open innovation was accelerated by the success of Proctor & Gamble's "Connect + Develop" model. Their leaders realized that for every P&G researcher, there were 200 scientists or engineers who were just as good in their areas, and that many of their best ideas had come from teams working across division boundaries. Top management support for this move was crucial, especially the endorsement by CEO A. G. Lafley, who set a goal that half the company's future new products would come from partners.

There is no right or wrong answer to the question of how far the innovation process should be opened, but the management team must decide. To gain an advantage and preempt competitors (who are attracted by the same logic) the firm has to invest in their partnering skills and collaborative digital platforms. The LEGO Ideas platform invites fans to submit concepts for new sets. The community of enthusiasts then votes on these ideas, and if there is enough support LEGO may develop the concept. The lucky few whose ideas are successfully launched (like the top-selling medieval blacksmith set) get 1% of the top-line revenue as their reward.

## Formulating a Growth Strategy

The process of making a strategy should iterate between the "outside-in" and "inside-out" perspectives.[14] These are not either-or ways of making a growth strategy but are complementary with one giving rise to the other. What really matters is where the process begins. Expansive strategy processes start with an "outside-in" perspective on present and prospective customers, competitors, and collaborators, by asking, "How are their needs and intentions changing?... What new competitors are poised to meet these new needs?... What are our rivals doing and plotting?" Seeing market realities through an outsider's eyes removes the firm from the constraints and biases of their direct experience.

An "inside-out" perspective has the firm's leaders looking outwards. Their questions are, "How can we sell more?... Gain additional market share?... Deploy our resources and capabilities?... Leverage our technology?" They are the counterparts to "what's possible," in our definition of innovation, but are most productive when they are linked to "what's needed" by the market.

An outside-in perspective respects but subordinates the inside-out factors within an expansive context. By using a wider lens, the leaders are also motivated to look farther into the future and consider the likely moves of all the players in their innovation ecosystem. This expansive perspective gives an objectivity (and appropriate skepticism) about the future that challenges comfortable assumptions and illusions.

*Summary.* The impetus given to the innovation flywheel by the full commitment to innovation by the leadership team is further boosted with clear and achievable ambitions for faster growth and a tolerance for the necessary risks of innovation. Growth leaders send their organizations clear expectations and directions through a growth strategy that communicates the goals for growth, the resources to be committed to achieving the growth ambitions, the arenas to be searched and the approach to be used to capture the growth opportunities.

CHAPTER 5

# Seeking Growth Opportunities

When opportunities to innovate are abundant, organic growth leaders capture better opportunities sooner than their reactive rivals and get them to market faster. These growth leaders have developed formidable capabilities[1] for capturing opportunities, by excelling with three linked processes: *searching* for potential opportunities, *screening* these opportunities for their market prospects and fit with the firm's strategy and capabilities, and then *selecting* the best alternatives to develop and launch. The searching process is the focus of this chapter, and the following chapter is about how to select the best opportunities.

Ideas for innovations abound in every company. A reactive approach will sweep up many possibilities: R&D will envision new prospects enabled by advances in technology; distributors, salespeople, and employees will suggest new customer solutions; there will be continuing pressure to match or leapfrog competitors by copying their innovations; and changes in strategy will need supporting innovations. While reactive sources of opportunities should always be encouraged, the odds of success from waiting and responding are much lower than if there is a disciplined search.

A directed, open, and systematic search for growth opportunities surfaces better opportunities and finds them faster than by waiting for them to emerge and then reacting. If a competitor finds and launches an

© The Author(s), under exclusive license to Springer Nature Switzerland AG 2025
G. S. Day, *Innovate to Grow*, Palgrave Executive Essentials,
https://doi.org/10.1007/978-3-031-77673-1_5

innovation sooner, it is much harder to catch up to them or gain an advantage. The set of opportunities will be further constrained if the search is limited to familiar places where innovation activity has always been focused. Organic growth leaders apply a more expansive, wider-spectrum approach to their search.

## A Wide-Spectrum Search for Opportunities

The familiar Ansoff matrix[2] was an early classification of the ways for a firm to find opportunities. This matrix proposed only four paths (market and product development, diversification, and market penetration), by contrasting existing versus new markets and products. In the six decades since there have been significant advances in our understanding of how firms can grow. These are better revealed with a wide-spectrum approach that begins by stretching and reimagining each dimension of the competitive strategy of a firm or business unit. This framework overcomes the narrowing impulses of habit, path dependency, and past commitments that produce reactive thinking.

This wide-spectrum approach to revealing innovation opportunities is undertaken by astute strategists taking an expansive view of the strategy of their firm. They apply their deeper insights into their customers, complementors, and collaborators and the underlying economic realities. These strategic thinkers also know that any product or service shortcomings (poor perceived value, overly constrained solutions, and lack of availability) are also opportunities to innovate.

A competitive strategy[3] is a set of activities for delivering a unique profile of value to customers. Superior firm performance is earned with customer value leadership, through maximizing the benefits that a target segment perceives from an offering while minimizing their perceived costs and risks. Most concepts of strategy distinguish the Customer Value Proposition (CVP) from the Business Model (BM) that taken together describes how the firm profitably fulfills the promise of the customer value proposition. Successful strategies require close synchronization of the CVP and an enabling Business Model, as shown in Fig. 5.1.

Expanding and reimagining each dimension of a firm's strategy gives the strategist eight broad avenues or directions for innovation. These are fed by the thirteen possible pathways shown in Fig. 5.2.

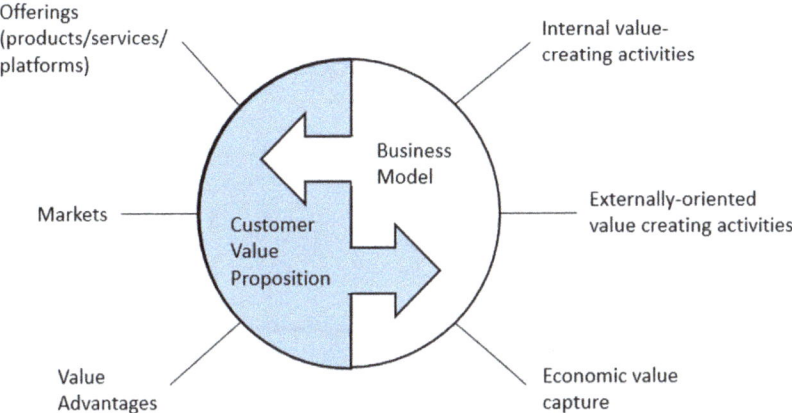

**Fig. 5.1** The dimensions of a strategy to be reimagined

## Pathways to Customer Value Innovations

A compelling value proposition should not be static: Innovations should rethink the offering, the current served market and the value profile showing the competitive advantages (and drawbacks) perceived by the customers in the target segments.

When continual market and technological turbulence becomes the new normal, it is healthier to be paranoid and keep watching over the horizon for looming threats to preempt or emerging opportunities to capture quickly. The challenge for leaders is not only to act faster but to act wisely. As the familiar adage "forewarned is forearmed" says, foresight prepares a firm to find opportunities sooner.

***Pathway 1.1: Satisfy latent customer needs.*** This pathway can be followed with the four steps in the design thinking process[4]: (1) empathize by deeply understanding the problems of the current or prospective customers, through observation by multi-disciplinary teams, (2) articulate these customer's emerging needs and problems, (3) ideate, and then (4) prototype a concept and test with users. This process assigns a central role to observational or ethnographic methods using skilled observers immersing themselves in the target customer's world. Many tools can be used to extract deep customer insights about their latent needs including: in-depth interviews, focus groups with users, structured listening, problem identification, and metaphor-elicitation methods. To

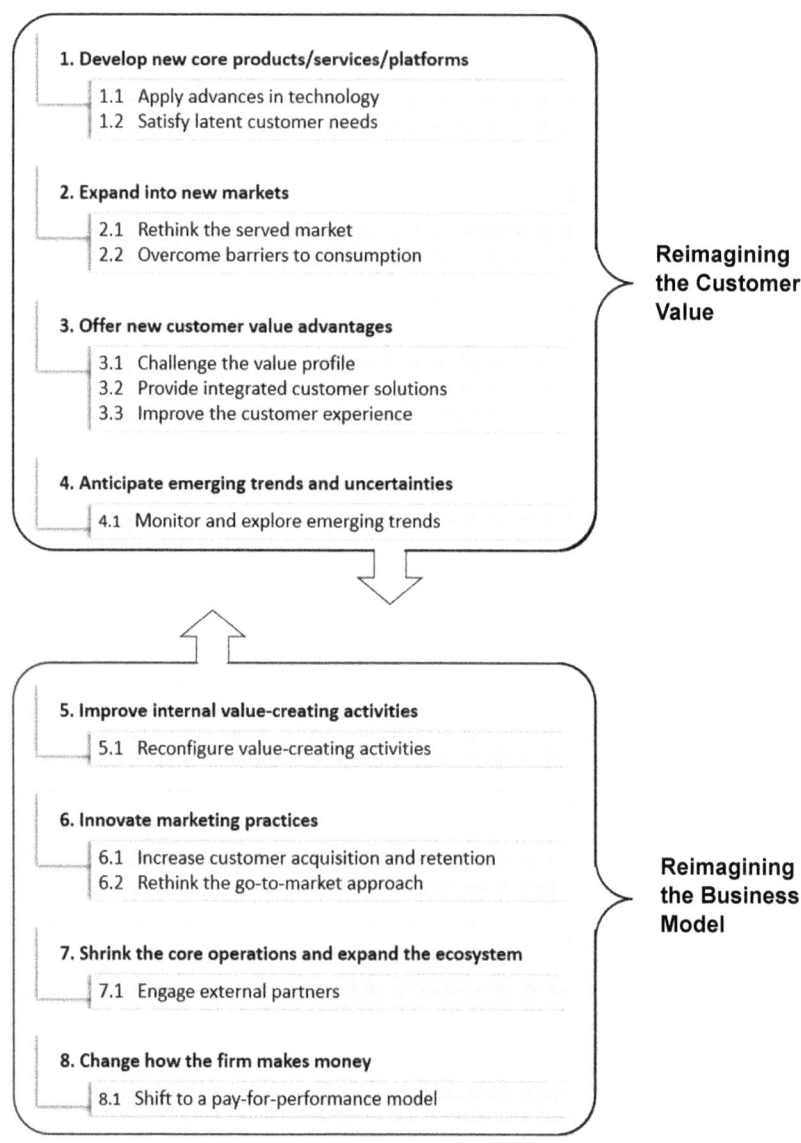

**Fig. 5.2** Innovation avenues and pathways

better hear the voices of their customers, a curious firm can also use these methods:

- **Leverage lead users.**[5] These are users who face needs in advance of the rest of the market and are working hard to find a solution sooner. Products such as correction fluid, sports bras, and Gatorade came from lead users (professional typists and elite athletes, respectively). In categories such as construction equipment or scientific test instruments, most innovations have come from alterations to products or workarounds made by these lead users.
- **Monitor complainers and defectors.** There is much to be learned by listening to unhappy customers, who express frustration when their needs are not met or understood.
- **Hunt for precursors in the parts of the country or globe where fads, fashions, or technology innovations appear earlier.** Companies such as the footwear-maker Converse use "cool hunters" and trend trackers as an early warning radar, to uncover emerging trends in clothing and shoes.

Lead user analysis is especially effective at capturing rich information about emerging needs. Another useful approach for gaining insights into underserved needs is the "elements of value model." There are 30 elements of value ranging from "reduces risk…connects…informs," to "self-actualization," that address four kinds of needs: functional, emotional, life changing, and social impact. The more elements of superior value provided by an innovation, the greater the customer's interest and the higher the firm's sustained top-line growth rate.

*Pathway 1.2: Apply advances in technology.* If any innovation is a combination of "what's possible" with "what's needed," then the release of Gen AI has transformed the technological possibilities. This breakthrough makes it possible to satisfy many more needs—sparking a surge of innovation opportunities to be captured by "someone." This should be the growth leader if they are alert but could be a laggard within the industry that sees a way to catch up, or perhaps an outsider from an adjacent sector using the new capabilities to avoid the existing barriers to entry. Thus, Gen AI can be a threat or an opportunity, depending on the ability of a firm to seize the possibilities.

Gen AI enables a firm to digest vast troves of unstructured data (of the sort residing in emails, project reviews, long buried consultant projects, or team platforms like Slack) and suggests intuitive answers to questions. A firm can extract new insights from their thousands of customer service conversations and distill them into actionable opportunities. Gen AI also encourages collective curiosity. The ease of answering questions permits deeper and better questions that sharply focus the collective imagination. This technology further democratizes curiosity if the leadership team permits wider access to proprietary databases. No longer can leaders say—as I have often heard—that "we don't know what we know" because their diffused knowledge is now accessible.

The formidable potential of Gen AI to energize opportunity capture can be seen in the $1.8 trillion global wellness market.[6] This market includes sleep, fitness, nutrition, nutrition and mindfulness. Wellness got a boost during the pandemic when people asked how they could keep themselves mentally and physically fit during their enforced isolation. These consumers' expectations have only increased, and they now demand more than a basic level of personalization.

Gen AI promises a much deeper level of individualization of wellness solutions using a rich array of personal biometric data. Consumers now have new tools for monitoring their health and wellness, creating even deeper pools of individual data to search for insights into maladies from headache disorders to autonomous disease. There is a strong latent "need" that can now be paired with technology solutions to generate new opportunities.

*Pathway 1.3: Innovative imitation.* Imitations may become winners, when they do more than just copy. The key is to understand the appeal of the original innovation and the barriers to its success, with an eye to making improvements in ways that customers will value. Thus, the iPod was not the first digital music player, and the iPhone was not the first smartphone. Apple took the original concepts and made them far more appealing and usable. Followers usually have lower R&D costs and face less risk of failure because the product concept has already been market tested. To succeed, they need to learn from the pioneer's problems and deploy an agile organization that can move fast to develop a better version before other competitors are tempted to follow.

This pathway is most successful when combined with the insights from pathway 4.1 ("Monitor and explore emerging trends"). Target Stores has mastered both capabilities. Their teams of merchants analyze search data, dissect trend reports, and survey customers for insights that are given to design teams. These capabilities enable Target to launch trendy brands that compete directly with well-known brands, but still feel fresh. Target was ready for the shift in apparel needs during the pandemic lockdowns with their activewear brand, All in Motion. Their line was affordably priced, trendy, and made from the latest performance fabrics. To support their strategy of innovative imitation they have invested in a 3D printing facility for prototyping, a lab for testing new products, and a sensory-testing facility.

*Pathway 2.1: Rethink the served markets.* This growth pathway is really a set of linked hiking routes starting from the same trailhead. Successfully traversing these routes demands a deep immersion into the differences between (a) the benefits sought by present and prospective customers, (b) the intensity of competitive rivalry in the prospective segment or geography, (c) the availability of channel intermediaries, and (d) the capabilities and financial resources available.

*Customer segment growth opportunities.* Customers sort themselves into benefit or choice segments by responding to what is offered in the product category. These are "what is" segments, in contrast with "might be" segments formed by overcoming the trade-offs and compromises some customers must make. This creative rethinking could be a pathway to the creation of a new sub-category. Warby-Parker challenged the established retail market for eyewear with an on-line channel that created a new customer segment and sub-category. Their prices were 75% below what optometrists charged to keep them affordable. To solve the problem of getting the right fit when a "try on" was not possible, they sent out five frames with glasses to be returned within five days at no charge.

*What are the prospects in adjacent geographies?* Until recently this was an attractive pathway, fueled by a steady advance in globalization (due to the increasing interconnectedness of the world economy). This interdependence of geographies and countries has continued to increase but has been slowed sharply by the forces of nationalism and protectionism, abetted by the populism that led to Brexit. Looking ahead, a likely outcome is the evolution of the global economy into regional trading blocs leaving fewer degrees of freedom to grow.

*Pathway 2.2: Overcome the barriers to consumption.* Non-consumers come in many guises. One group seems close to your currently served customers. They may purchase the industry's offerings occasionally but could become enthusiastic customers if there is a superior alternative.

Perhaps they are only buying because they have to; think about health insurance or taxicab users before Uber. Satisfying these non-consumers starts by deeply understanding the value they are seeking and their pain points. The fast-food chain Pret A Manger succeeded by doing just that. They offered restaurant-quality sandwiches made fresh daily, using superior ingredients, and ready to grab and go.

A more difficult group of non-consumers to satisfy are not necessarily uninterested, but encounter barriers to purchasing and consuming[7]:

1. **Lack of money.** Existing alternatives are too expensive.
2. **Lack of skills.** Existing alternatives are too complex, requiring expert guidance or lots of training.
3. **Lack of access.** Available alternatives can be consumed only in specific contexts, locations, and so on.
4. **Lack of time.** Finding and consuming the available alternatives takes too long.

*Pathway 3.1 Challenge the Value Profile.* This pathway gained traction with the popularity of "Blue Ocean Strategy."[8] To find a potential blue ocean or an untapped market space, start with a value profile of the varying levels of features offered by the incumbents and ask: Which features can be eliminated? Reduced below industry standards? Raised above industry standards? Which features could be created that have never been offered?

This pathway was used to conceive the Ginger budget hotel chain, launched in India by the Tata Group. This chain was designed to meet the needs of frequent business travelers who wanted a place to stay that was not as earthy or unpredictable as a low-price hotel but wouldn't pay the prices of a five-star hotel. The Ginger brand promised a customer experience that was "consistent, simple, light-hearted" at the best price. Their small rooms were strictly no-frills, with dorm-style furniture, but with state-of-the-art, new mattresses to ensure a good night's sleep. Costs were tightly controlled by locating the hotels in business districts away from high-cost real estate, using a self-check in routine, and employing minimal staff. The Ginger hotels offered a value profile to the target segment that closely met their needs.

***Pathway 3.1: Provide more complete solutions.*** Four criteria must be satisfied if a solution is to create value for customers that is more than the sum of the parts:

1. It is co-created with customers.
2. It is tailored to each customer's requirements.
3. It delivers superior service on the customer's terms, including rapid response, ready access, and clear accountability from the supplier.
4. Some of the risk perceived by customers is absorbed by suppliers through performance- or risk-based contracts or commitments.

It is wrong to offer a bundle of available products that enables one-stop shopping as a "solution." These are not innovations and competitors can copy them easily and so they do not typically result in growth. Growth comes from solutions based on outside-in insights about how to solve a customer's problems.

The British cyber security firm Sophos learned that most of their customers were struggling to coordinate security across multiple endpoints (lap-tops, mobile phones, tablets, IOS software, Android software, etc.) while the regulations were constantly changing. These customers also lacked deep knowledge of the incessant cyber threats from hacking, or how to maintain a secure network across their diverse endpoints. To meet this pressing need Sophos created industry-targeted sets of components that secured both networks and devices. They were easier to deploy because they were designed to work together. With a cost-effective and simpler solution, Sophos was able to serve the medium to small enterprise companies that could not afford complex solutions.

***Pathway 3.3: Improve the customer experience.*** Each purchase decision by a customer, from installing a medical device to choosing and staying at a hotel, has a distinct beginning, middle, and end, with many steps along the way that stretch over time. The key to innovating on this pathway is to first capture the complete customer experience from the customer's perspective—not what you hoped or expected the customer to experience. There are many ways to map a customer's experience or journey. Methods that also capture the emotional state of the customer during their journey are the most useful. Are they feeling "great...neutral...or upset" at each step of their journey?

Once all the steps are mapped, new customer value can be created by asking which steps in the process could be opportunities for improvement:

- Which steps can be improved? Westin Hotels created the "Heavenly Experience" after interviews and observations of people getting ready for bed revealed the importance that business travelers gave to having a good night's sleep.
- Which steps can be eliminated, combined in a different order, or made smarter? Can the burden on the customer be automated, or shifted elsewhere?
- Where are the pain points?
- What factors dictate which choice alternatives are included in the consideration set?
- Where can time delays be eliminated?

With an outside-in view of what the customer sees, hears, feels, and does, companies can improve their existing offering or find white space opportunities.

The disruption of the customer experience with frozen yogurt in 2010 demonstrates the possibilities for innovation. When TCBY ("The Country's Best Yogurt") was in ascendance, the customer went to a counter and a server assembled a yogurt cup using pre-measured portions and then charged for each topping. In the early 2000s TCBY had nearly 1800 stores. By 2021 they were reduced to 300 struggling stores—replaced by a customer self-service model pioneered by Pinkberry. In their model the customer first chooses and pours the flavor of yogurt they prefer into a cup, decides how much of each topping to add, and pays by total weight at the check-out counter. This model has taken over the sector. The lesson here is that customers want to be in control of their purchase journey. An obvious point, perhaps, with powerful implications.

*Pathway 4: Anticipate emerging trends and issues.* Some firms are adept at anticipating and exploiting the opportunities created by rapid technological advances and rapid changes in their markets, while others struggle to see the potential and react. The contrast between the vigilant and vulnerable firms was accentuated during the pandemic. A vigilant sensing capability is enhanced by two inter-related learning processes: *peripheral vision* for the detection of weak signals from the boundaries of the organization, and *vigilant learning* that interprets these signals and explores their implications.[9] When uncertainty intensifies, these learning processes are strengthened with tools such as scenario planning that create narratives about alternative plausible futures. (These narratives focus managerial attention while expanding the shared mental model of possibilities.) Scenarios are also useful ways to widen the vision of the leadership team and anticipate changes along other pathways.

### *Pathways to Business Model Innovation*

This set of innovation pathways starts from the inside-out by posing four questions about the existing system for *creating and delivering* customer value, and *capturing* some of that value: (1) What activities need to be carried out? (2) How should these activities be sequenced and connected? (3) Who carries out each activity? And (4) How will value be captured?

A business model is a purposeful weaving together of many interdependent activities. Some activities will be performed by the firm and others by suppliers, partners, or customers and combined in a myriad of ways to create a rich set of possibilities. These dictated the strategic choices made by a European start-up with a breakthrough in friction-reduction technology that could be applied to any product with moving parts. Once a target customer segment, such as automobiles, was selected as the best opportunity, there were many further choices to be made. Should they build machines that embedded and exploited their technology? Operate a job-shop to perform surface treatment for partners? License the technology to third parties such as machine tool makers? Each of these business model choices required a different set of capabilities, either within the firm or beyond it, and established the prices, operating margins, risk exposure, and profit potential. Once a choice is made it is hard to reverse, and constrains future strategic moves.

***Pathway 5.1: Reconfigure the value-creating activities.*** The ZARA apparel chain, a pioneer of the "fast fashion" concept, totally rethought their design and manufacturing processes. At most clothing makers the value-creation process starts with designers, who plan collections as much as a year in advance, and requires long lead times and manufacturing in Asia to contain costs.

ZARA innovated their business model in many ways. First, they monitor fashion trends continuously to guide their in-house designers, who then fashion what is currently hot. These designs are sent to company-owned factories in Spain, where just-in-time systems can move a blouse, dress, or coat from the drawing board to a store in less than a month. Because Zara is more attuned to the latest fashions, it can change more often and avoids the profit drain from marking down large inventories.

*Anticipating advances in technology*. Many business model innovations are prompted and enabled by advances in technologies—especially digital transformations that make it possible to combine and coordinate activities and provide new functions. For example, platform business models such as the ride-sharing app pioneered by Uber, improve the rider's experience by quickly integrating the activities and requests of thousands of drivers and riders. It's never easy to get the timing of an advance in technology right. Being too early alerts rivals to the possibilities and the pioneer absorbs most of the risk of development. The shipping giant, Maersk Line waited twenty years before adopting containerization. They wanted standards to be set and for the technology to mature, before moving decisively by building larger ships and modern port facilities, to fully capture the opportunity.

**Pathway 6.2: Enhance the go-to-market approach.** The convention in business model thinking that separates value creation from value delivery activities is misleading at best. The go-to-market approach should also contribute considerable customer value. An effective sales team provides useful information, diagnoses problems, and works with the customer to create an integrated solution (thus implementing pathway 5).

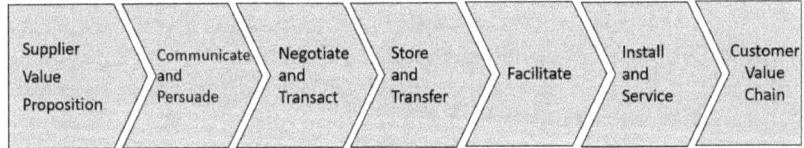

This pathway begins with communication and persuasion activities. In 2012 Nike's CEO presciently observed that "Connecting [with customers] used to be, 'Here's some product and here's some advertising; we hope you like it'...Connecting today is a dialogue." His view explains Nike's shift in its marketing efforts. Nike's money is now going to online activities, social media, and communities of users with common interests. Some of this helps insulate Nike from celebrity endorsements going wrong. It also delivers meaningful customer value by improving the customer's (whether a runner, basketball player, or couch potato) experience, and keeps Nike ahead of rivals.

There is potential for growth-enhancing innovation in every activity a firm takes to reach, persuade, and fulfill customer requirements. Some of these innovations respond to the growing complexity of customer solutions, and the need to rethink the role of the traditional sales force in an era of ubiquitous access to information. This rethink was accelerated during the pandemic, when B2B customers switched to online methods for searching, talking with suppliers, and transacting routine orders.

The theme in retail and consumer goods markets is "omnichannel," the popular term for seamlessly integrating online and offline shopping activities. These coordinated channels span the physical and digital environments to include channels that are not controlled by the firm. These shifts, plus the ability of consumer goods companies to analyze customer journey data with Gen AI to better understand consumer choices, present a myriad of opportunities for innovation.

***Pathway 8: Change how the firm makes money.*** The ultimate business model question is "How will the firm capture some of the value it provides to customers? How does the company get paid for the value it creates?" There have been dramatic changes in how many industries answer this question. For some firms, these changes have been involuntary. The media industry has struggled to innovate how firms make money in an era of easy downloads and file sharing. While many customers are abandoning the traditional "cable package," neither the firms that produce entertainment (such as HBO) nor the firms that deliver it (such as Comcast) have been able to innovate an "a la carte" approach, which customers clearly want, while making enough money to sustain themselves.

One of the most dramatic innovations of the value-capture system is the change from a product-sale model to a subscription model. Today one can lease an industrial carpet as easily as a copier. Service models are not just about leasing. Praxair captures the increased value of providing gases to the point of use in a factory, rather than just delivering a tank car. Castrol Industrial devised a way to share gains from reducing the use of its products, based on advice it gave to a client. The firm now captures this increased value by advising its customers on how to buy *less* product. The Israeli firm Netafim—a market leader in drip-irrigation systems—couldn't persuade smaller farmers to pay to install their expensive systems. Netafim overcame this resistance by offering farmers a free installed system with periodic maintenance, to be paid for from a share of each farmer's increased crop yields. They could afford to do this, because the risks for the firm could be managed with their deeper knowledge, and ability to spread the risk. If the system failed at one farm, Netafim could make up for it elsewhere.

## Many Pathways to Growth

Curves Fitness Center[10] became the largest fitness and health club franchise in the world by challenging the value profiles of full-service health clubs. These traditional health clubs catered to men and women and offered a full range of equipment for a high monthly fee. Curves was positioned as a women's gym, providing a total body workout in 30 minutes at one-third of the monthly fee. Its equipment was especially designed for women and arranged in a circle to encourage conversation; timed music moved participants from machine to machine in a way that made the overall experience enjoyable.

The main growth pathway followed by Curves was the delivery of a different profile of attributes that departed from traditional full-service health clubs. But they also overcame barriers to consumption among women and better satisfied their latent or unmet needs for a disciplined workout with social reinforcement. Curves also offers a deeper lesson: The more growth pathways involved with an innovation initiative, the more compelling and integrated the value proposition, and the harder it is for rivals to copy.

This chapter poses a strategic choice that is usually implicit: either take a *reactive* approach and wait for opportunities to arrive, or *systematically* probe each of the twelve growth pathways to identify the best opportunities and pursue them ahead of others. Growth leaders take a disciplined approach to the twelve pathways that balance *divergence*—to widen the search for the best opportunities—with *convergence* on those that best serve the growth strategy. How they converge faster on better opportunities to develop is the theme of the next chapter.

CHAPTER 6

# Deciding Which Opportunities to Capture

Selecting the best opportunities to capture seems to be a straight-forward resource allocation problem. Because money, people and time resources are always scarce, most firms want to use them for their most promising projects. This logic has led many leadership teams to wrongly apply the same analytical frameworks they would use to evaluate any other capital project, like investing in a new IT system, plant or office building. These tools tell them to select only the few opportunities that promise to generate more economic value than other investments, with the usual adjustments for riskiness and time. They then fall into the trap of using familiar discounted cash flow or internal rates of return to rank and then select among growth opportunities. The emphasis is on their financial attractiveness.

Familiar financial analysis techniques are not equipped to deal with the uncertainty of innovation opportunities: Will there be a market? Will the technologies work at scale? How will the competitors react? What will be the trajectory of prices when competitors enter? Decisions to proceed with any growth opportunity are based on scarce hard information and require experienced judgment to weigh the many imponderables. The process of assembling incomplete information and asking difficult "what if?" and "what about?" questions is usually drawn-out and often inconclusive. This is fertile ground for the intervention of cognitive biases[1] that distort the decision process.

Topping the list of biases that distort decisions to capture an opportunity is *anchoring* on a target breakeven number or discounted cash flow ROI. It is tempting to start with this target and adjust key cost, price, and adoption parameters to deliver the desired result. A second culprit is *gamesmanship*. Resource allocation is often framed as a zero-sum game, with "worthy" projects competing for the same scarce pool of investment dollars. Since most managers are confident their project is as good as the others, they rally a set of overly optimistic assumptions to support their case. Many other biases come into play. A favorite is the *confirmation bias*, where we select and embrace information that supports our beliefs and assumptions and reject or ignore uncomfortable information that challenges these assumptions. This bias is exacerbated by *overconfidence*, making us far too certain that our current assumptions are correct. Finally, development teams are susceptible to *groupthink*, in which all the members in a group learn to see the world the same way.

Firms with confidence in their ability to innovate, recognize these ingrained biases, and deal with them in several ways. First, they are unflinching in their postmortems of failures or disappointments and look for patterns in their assumptions that went consistently awry. Usually these are assumptions about less controllable market factors such as rate of market adoption, market share, or the trajectory of prices over time. These postmortems are motivated by a desire to learn, and not a thinly disguised search for someone to blame. The lessons are codified and added to the collective intelligence of the firm.

Growth leaders apply the lessons learned from their successes and disappointments through three successively tighter filters, to converge on the best opportunities to capture.[2] They begin their convergence by refining their initial set of prospects with heuristics or simple rules that use the lessons from their past experience to focus on their best opportunities. Next, they use a rigorous screening framework to surface and test their assumptions about market prospects and product feasibility. This filter determines whether an opportunity warrants further development or should be dropped. The third filter narrows the set of opportunities further by investing in real options to cut the cost of failure. These three filters overlap by posing the same fundamental questions with increasing rigor, specificity, and thoroughness. The process of applying them is learned through experience and shared throughout the firm. It is flexible enough to reveal any unanticipated opportunities that might emerge during the learning process. There should always be room for serendipity in innovation.

## REFINING THE OPPORTUNITY SET

Growth leaders have developed heuristics[3] or simple rules to refine a large set of opportunities. These heuristics provide a threshold level of structure—with room for discretion—by putting constraints in place. In the early 2000s, the Corning Inc. leadership team set an ambitious goal of doubling the number of major new businesses to be started in the next decade. They created a set of simple rules they had learned from their past successes: They would only consider markets promising more than $500 million in potential revenue while leveraging the firm's expertise in material sciences and be a critical component in a complex system.

Opportunity-capturing heuristics[4] are valuable because they provide: (1) Boundary rules—which opportunities should not be pursued? (2) Selection rules—how should opportunities be selected and prioritized? (3) "How-to" rules—how are the selected opportunities to be processed? (4) Timing rules—when will these opportunities be executed? and then, (5) Exit rules—when should work on a prospective opportunity be stopped?

Heuristics help to focus scarce organizational energy and enthusiasm toward high potential opportunities. The experience of the LEGO Group shows why this matters. In the late 1990s the company launched ill-advised forays into video games, theme parks, and learning centers in search of new play experiences. Many of these opportunities lost so much money that they pushed the LEGO Group close to bankruptcy. New leadership overcame these setbacks by adopting heuristics or simple rules that refocused their innovation activities on the traditional play experience it was already known for, while limiting the pursuit of other experiences.

*Fast and frugal* heuristics are usually adequate to bound and shape the complex processes for capturing opportunities. They are tailored to each firm and evolve from what they learned through direct experience and their observation of the best practices of other firms. The following heuristics came from my interviews with members of their leadership teams and then were confirmed with content analyses of internal documents and observations of their strategic choices.[5]

*Combine reinforcing growth pathways that will deter followers.* The reach and ambition of innovations along each of the growth pathways described in the previous chapter can vary from the minor and incremental to the major and disruptive breakthrough. The variety of possible combinations of pathways seems daunting but also encouraging, because equity markets reward the promise of an (economic) value-adding variety of innovation initiatives. This is grounds for optimism for any firm whose growth is lagging. It is unlikely that all the best combinations have been explored and exploited.

The value of innovating along several reinforcing pathways is demonstrated by Adobe, Inc.'s digital bet on cloud-based storage. By 2009 the growth prospects for their flagship product, the image editing program Photoshop, were sluggish and the growing ubiquity of smartphones allowed people to manage their own photos. Also looming on the horizon was a steep decline in the cost of cloud computing storage, giving a potential opening to deep-pocketed rivals like Google or Microsoft to possibly enter their photo editing market. The leaders at Adobe, Inc. saw this potential threat as an opportunity to innovate.

In late 2011, Adobe shifted from selling boxed software on a floppy disc (giving users a perpetual license) to a cloud-based subscription service. By May 2013 they stopped providing periodic upgrades for boxed software programs and replaced them with continuous software improvements available only via the cloud. This freed the company to make continuous improvements to their software, rather than delaying any changes and improvements for months to await the next software release.

The growth pathways followed by Adobe, Inc. show how to capture an opportunity and then create further growth pathways that were once out of reach. Figure 6.1 maps the sequence of reinforcing pathways they followed to build big barriers to imitation by their potential rivals and successfully change their strategy.

*Think differently.* Conventional industry wisdom and established practice are predictable but can also be constraining. Diagnostics firms will apply the latest advances in sensor technology to develop their new devices, and consumer packaged goods companies look for opportunities for incremental product improvements (along with forays into new geographic markets). Because the dominant pathway for an industry is also the essence of the value proposition it warrants the most resources. Momentum, past experience and the need to match the moves of rivals reinforce this conventional wisdom. Because this industry-wide belief

6  DECIDING WHICH OPPORTUNITIES TO CAPTURE    73

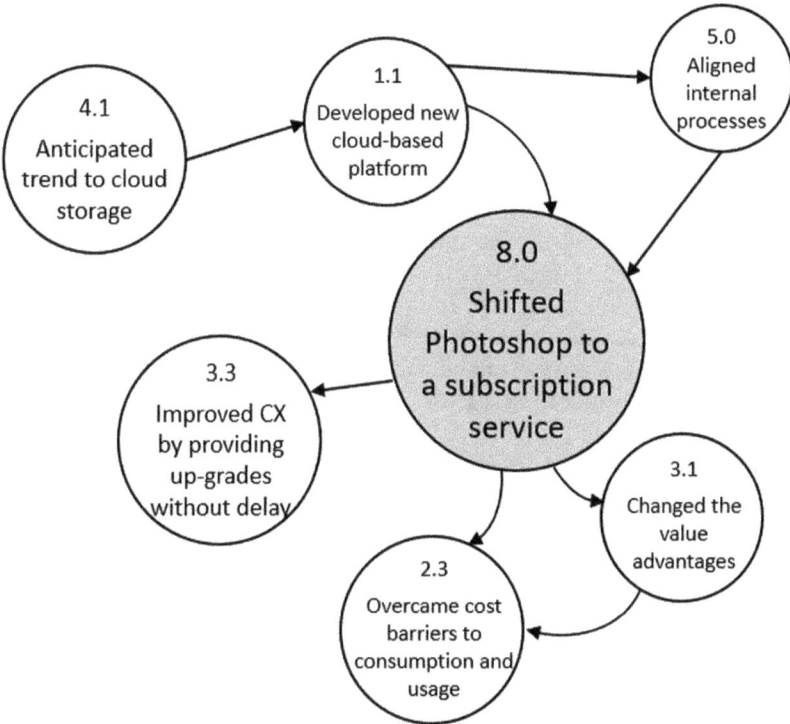

**Fig. 6.1** Adobe's innovation pathways

system is deeply embedded in the minds of experienced leaders, it usually limits the exercise of imagination and fuels a confirmation bias. Deliberately thinking differently helps to overcome this form of myopia and surface attractive innovations that are hard to copy.

Novartis Pharmaceuticals took advantage of the powerful inertia behind the traditional go-to-market model used throughout their industry. This familiar model sent armies of sales representatives to "detail" prescribing doctors with one-way communications of the therapeutic benefits of a new drug. Every sales representative followed the same carefully constructed script and left a standard set of collateral materials.

In 2012 Novartis leadership devised an innovative sales model to help their 25,000 sales representatives in 80 countries engage with doctors in consultative, two-way dialogues. Value-added services and wide channels of communication replaced the stale recitation of standardized messages. Each sales representative was given a mobile device that enabled video conferencing with experts, while accessing the latest digital information and interactive patient tools. Their reps could immediately access whatever data the doctor would find most relevant to their patients.

This digital physician engagement platform also captured detailed information about the sales interaction and improved the understanding of the customer's needs. As Novartis deepened its market knowledge the company was able to spot budding problems and possible market opportunities much faster than competitors. While some of their competitors used digital sale tools, these were usually used to support rather than supplant the conventional detailing model, leaving their reps far less engaged with a prescribing doctor.

*Preempt potential threats.* A business model innovation was used by Dow Corning, the global leader in silicone-based materials, for preemption. Their traditional strategy of providing high-touch design services coupled with personalized sales support and order-size flexibility for its customers, was threatened because a growing number of their price-sensitive buyers were asking for the same high quality and reliability, with lower prices for the standardized items they were buying. This opened the market to low-cost offshore competitors.

To protect their position in this emerging price-sensitive market segment, Dow-Corning built a low-cost business model tailored to the needs of the fast-growing price-sensitive segment, within a new and very lean separate organization they called XIAMETER. Sales and distribution costs were slashed by eliminating technical service, lengthening delivery times from hours to days, and limiting order-size flexibility and eliminating customer education. The new company had only an online ordering system with all communication done solely by email. This move succeeded and the erstwhile new competitors were forced to retrench.

*Embrace anomalies.* An anomaly is something that deviates from what is normal or expected. Growth leaders seek market anomalies as early indicators of opportunities. Intuit calls this *Savoring the Surprise*. When they realized that some users of their online money management service Mint weren't behaving the way the young-professional target market was "supposed" to behave, they dug deeper and found that these users had adopted Mint to manage their self-employment income and spending. Many were Uber or Lyft drivers, operating in the expanding gig economy. Embracing this market insight, Intuit designed a variation of QuickBooks for self-employed workers—which became its fastest-growing product. This novel product extension opportunity would not have surfaced had Intuit not been open to an anomaly.

Growth leaders use their heuristics to limit their search to high-yield places to look while keeping their eyes open to serendipitous possibilities within their search field. In this exploratory sprit they regularly ask, "Is this an instructive precursor to what may be coming to our market? What does it say to us?" To find these precursors and spark their collective curiosity, they may put outposts in markets where innovations often appear first.

## Screening for Learning: Selecting Opportunities to Capture

The process for screening opportunities to develop further is as much about learning more about a market opportunity and calibrating the risks as deciding to make a go or no-go decision. A decision to proceed is based on a myriad of assumptions, and each is shrouded in uncertainty about the future.

Growth leaders select their opportunities with a comprehensive screening framework that surfaces the assumptions that will determine success and validating those that matter most. This is a learning process for narrowing the zone of uncertainty to a manageable level. Valuable lessons are learned when shortenings and flaws are revealed and need to be corrected before the project is advanced further.

Here are some innocuous—but potentially dangerous assumptions—that need to be surfaced, challenged, and then validated:

- Customers will buy our new device/product/system because of the technically advanced features.
- We can complete development on time and within the budget.
- Competitors won't react.
- Key influencers will support us.

### *An Valuable Screening Framework*

Growth leaders probe any opportunity with a sequence of penetrating but straight-forward questions.[6] At the highest level these questions are:

Is the opportunity *real*—can anyone make it, and is there a market? Can we *win* with our concept and the resources of our firm? Is *it worth doing* from a financial and strategic perspective? This is a sequential screening process, because each question should be answered before asking the next. There are many layers of questions for probing deeply into critical details. The first three layers are shown in Fig. 6.2. This R-W-W screen should not be viewed as a GO—KILL tool imposed by management; otherwise learning will be subverted and manipulated by the project team. Instead, it is an effective way to surface crucial assumptions and knowledge gaps to be closed, before a credible business case can be made.

Because the members of the evaluation team may be both evaluators and advocates, screening of opportunities is susceptible to misuse and manipulation. Team members' convictions about the merits of the

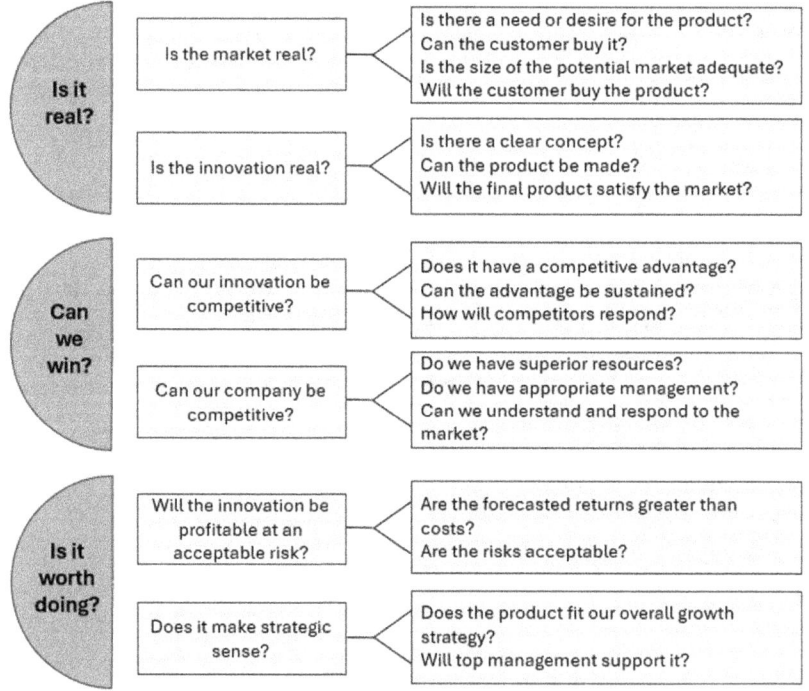

**Fig. 6.2** Screening for learning

project may lead them to make cursory evaluations if they fear that a deep assessment, including the frank voicing of doubts might imperil the project. One way to eliminate this potential pitfall is to enlist a credible outside facilitator. The best candidate is someone from another part of the company with a solid track record of innovation, good instincts, and no stake in the outcome. This person's role should be to expose the key assumptions, information gaps and differences of opinion, and then work with the evaluation team to resolve them.

When most of the assumptions have been surfaced, the next step is to classify each by importance and confidence.[7] The priority matrix shown below in (Fig. 6.3) identifies which assumptions must be validated, and which can be taken as given because they are probably not material .

Some opportunities have such glaring flaws that they can be easily discarded. Others may be attractive if the assumptions are supported. This is a drawn-out learning process, informed by surveys and rapid prototyping with target consumers, experiments in test markets, and deep competitor intelligence about their development projects. Seldom is this screening step completely conclusive; always leaving some residual uncertainty to be understood better through a real options lens.

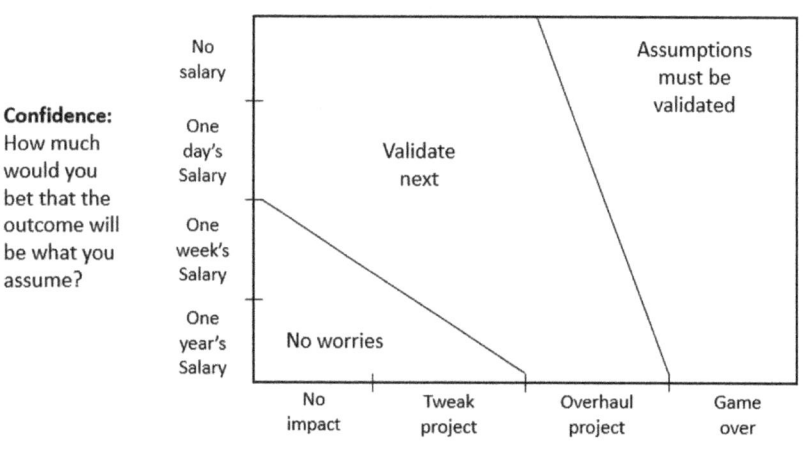

Fig. 6.3 Prioritizing assumptions

***Real options.*** are relatively small investments that create the right-but not an obligation-to make further investments as the future unfolds.[8] There has to be asymmetry in the distribution of returns, with greater upside potential than downside exposure to failure and loss. This happens when you can terminate the investment or otherwise contain any negative outcomes while retaining the right to make further investments should the initial foray seem promising. The next step depends entirely on what is learned.

By keeping real options open, an innovation team will focus more on cutting the cost of an early failure versus trying to reduce the rate of failure. Some ways to maximize the learning are small scale pilots to prove the manufacturing process before scaling up, and toehold investments in start-ups with an option to buy a larger stake later. Real options thinking also requires an accounting for follow-on growth opportunities that would not be possible unless you launched the new initiative. These are often valued at zero, because they may not be realized. In my view this is dangerous, because it disadvantages the growth initiative. A healthier approach is to run a realistic NPV for the new venture, and if it falls short of some (risk-adjusted) threshold rate of return, you ask how much future cash flow would have to be realized from the exercise of the growth option for the investment to be attractive.

## Tightening Innovation Discipline

Innovation capabilities and resources are most productive when they are used to capture the best opportunities. Paradoxically, most firms take an undisciplined and reactive approach to their search for innovative opportunities. They are usually slower to grasp these opportunities, thus limiting their degrees of freedom to probe, experiment, and learn about innovations that might drive their organic growth rate higher.

Growth leaders seek their opportunities strategically and gain a readiness advantage by capturing them sooner while being ready to act when the time is right. The office furniture maker Herman Miller used their deep insights into office design and anticipated that employees would need to have more autonomy to shape their own workplace when the global pandemic abated. The company created a clever "un-system" of furniture that was meant to be moved easily on demand—pushed into groups or pulled away for solo work—without getting approval or needing help.

All firms are challenged by the rapid proliferation of innovation opportunities created by market changes and technological advances along many fronts. Organic growth leaders use their own heuristics to manage their deluge of opportunities. Their "fast-and-frugal" heuristics help their leadership teams to make rapid decisions that are good enough and conserve and focus their scarce attention resources.

CHAPTER 7

# Accomplishing the Work of Innovation

Declaring an ambition to grow faster doesn't tell employees what they should do to achieve their firm's growth goals. This direction is given through the fourth discipline of accomplishment through an innovation work system that encourages the necessary behaviors, within an organization climate that can support essential innovation activities.

Sustained accomplishment of the work of innovation requires a supportive culture. This culture represents the shared values, norms, and beliefs about appropriate or expected behavior. There are no growth leaders with shallow or forgettable cultures. They don't use slogans such as *"share to gain... fail fast... always work for a win–win"* that reflect a faith in best practices; instead, they create innovative work practices to keep ahead of technology and market changes.

The legendary LEGO Group, often called "The Apple of Toys" devised a new way of working to keep up with accelerating digitalization.[1] They used digital technologies to speed the shift to open innovation, with the LEGO Ideas platform hosting a community of more than 2.8 million users that has shared and debated 135,000 ideas for Lego sets. By 2017 their durable brick sets were becoming more digital, with games, virtual reality, and an interactive website.

To innovate further with these digital products, they moved from a traditional functional structure in favor of more agile cross-functional teams. Tasks originated with the program managers who laid out the high-level outcomes needed to achieve their goals. This created projects that might consist of new features, updates, or user stories. The goal was to have a testable result within two weeks. Allocating the work was done every two months with a meeting of all the teams that were described as "planning as a social event." The working teams were loosely specialized but had enough functional expertise to complete their work.

During their planning sessions, each team identified the risks that might cause their projects to fail and the key dependencies among the tasks to be resolved. This was the input to a leadership review of their many projects and a deep discussion of tradeoffs and risks to be resolved. In this way leadership showed they were deeply engaged in the work of innovation and became better informed about the possibilities.

LEGO Group's global sales reached $9.65 billion in 2023, while growing much faster than rivals Mattel and Hasbro. There are now 400 billion bricks in the world (equivalent to 86 bricks for each person). Yet people continue to buy more LEGO kits and experiences, because of their continuous mastery of innovation that appeals to an ever-expanding fan base reached by gaming and movie platforms.

## Growth Enabling Narratives

An innovation narrative is the story told by the organization about innovation and how it occurs—or doesn't—within the firm.[2] These stories reveal the governing beliefs and help explain past performance. As I shared in Chapter 2 there are two kinds of narratives about innovation. Growth leaders share an up-beat growth-enabling story, while growth laggards are likely to share a defensive story that undermines their innovation initiatives.

Further insight comes by asking the leadership team "Are you confident that the company's organic growth goals can be reached? Why?" and "Are those goals usually hit or missed? Why?" It is crucial to understand what executives are really saying when they answer. Are they rationalizing the company's past innovation performance? Are they ascribing that performance to factors and forces outside their control? Those responses signal a defensive posture, which can easily undermine growth. But if the leaders take responsibility for missed goals and say what they are changing to improve future results, they are poised to affirm growth. Then the narrative their answers suggest should be tested with an in-depth analysis of a sampling of the company's innovation initiatives. No narrative should be taken at face value.

If the prevailing innovation narrative in your company is growth-denying and impeding innovation, you can start to change it by envisioning a desired future state in which the company has become an industry leader in organic growth through innovation. Answering these questions will also help: If our organization acted out a growth-affirming narrative, what behaviors would we see? What would a storyboard showing "the way innovation works around here" look like? With a growth-affirming narrative in mind, you can turn your attention to bringing it to life within the company.

In 2013, Philadelphia-based Jefferson University and its associated hospital system hired a new president and CEO, who was dedicated to innovation and organizational transformation throughout the 194-year-old institution. Soon after Dr. Stephen Klasko arrived, he convened focus groups, town halls, and email contests to enlist roughly 1000 of the health system's employees to craft an organizational narrative placing innovation front and center.

Here's how Klasko viewed their innovation aspirations: *We will innovate to bring care and caring to where the patient is. We will become an entrepreneurial health organization, bringing creativity, passion, and flexibility along with the more traditional academic medical center skill sets of strategy, focus, and discipline... Thomas Jefferson University will concentrate on emerging health professions—it will provide the people needed in health care 10 years from now.*

He next filled many senior positions, which had been purposely left open by the board, with executives committed to innovation. He also appointed a new leader for what he called the "strategic pillar of innovation," who was one of his four direct reports. And he established an ongoing, yearlong executive education program for high potential employees, to equip the next generation of leaders with tools for managing rapid innovation. The hospital system has improved top-line revenue from $1.5 Billion in 2014 to $9.7 Billion in 2024, with several large acquisitions, and organic growth of 5% per year in outpatient revenue and 3% annual growth for inpatient revenue.

## The Work of Innovation

Innovation work is accomplished with eight organizational levers acting together to realize a growth-enabling narrative. The aim should be the creation of a supportive work setting where the arrangement of tasks, governance, and resources focuses individual effort toward superior innovation results.[3]

The eight levers shown in Fig. 7.1 become the work environment that innovation teams adapt to over time. Pulling on these levers in a coherent, coordinated way changes the work environment people experience as they go about their innovation activities. They will naturally adapt their activities to fit this changed work environment.

**Fig. 7.1** The eight levers of a work system

An uncoordinated approach or inconsistent focus will yield episodic and late innovation results. Be careful not to confuse "making innovation routine" with routinizing innovation. Routinizing innovation does not work. Strict application of standard "lean" or Six Sigma processes to innovation activities may even constrain and obstruct innovation activities.[4] Making innovation routine also means embedding a supportive work system within the DNA of the firm. Then the stories people share about innovation communicate the successful exercise of curiosity and leverage discoveries to stimulate further innovation.

### *Innovating the Work of Innovation*

A leadership team wanting to improve how their organization innovates starts with a strong commitment to the four innovation disciplines. This is how Proctor & Gamble[5] transformed itself from a slow, cumbersome and siloed organization in 2016 to achieve organic growth leadership in 2023. The change initiative was led by Kathy Fish, the Chief Research, Development and Innovation Officer, who had previously orchestrated the shift from big, centralized project teams to a decentralized model with 150 small teams within ten business units.

She began by studying which innovation practices had resulted in products with "irresistible superiority" in the past. Then she developed a convincing narrative about a future in which P&G delivered a customer experience so much better than competitors, that it was indeed "irresistible." At its core, this meant forging long-term relationships with its target consumers. Functional superiority was not enough; the innovation had to make an emotional connection. This newly envisioned future had P&G exploring many smaller scale innovations within and across business units, conducted in close collaboration with consumers, and driven by their problems and needs. It was clear to her that P&G had to work each of their organizational levers differently, and especially the following:

1. **Organizational structure:** Two or three members of a dedicated, multi-functional team pursued "fast cycle, inexpensive experimentation … around a consumer problem or 'opportunity' space." An influential business unit senior leader served as Executive Sponsor to facilitate group work including breaking down silo barriers. Each business unit had a Growth Board composed of the business unit President and key VPs. These leaders owned the innovation process

and the innovation portfolio, assessed what had been learned and decided which initiatives deserved funding. At the corporate level an Enterprise Growth Board oversaw P&G's total innovation portfolio.
2. **Development processes:** A fast-to-fail, lean process had five stages: discover opportunity areas; generate ideas; validate the problem, solution and business model; incubate and scale up. Their Governance lever guided stair-step investments and funding to each stage in this innovation development process: low investments through the validation stage; larger investments during concept development and product testing stages and the highest investments should an innovation make it to the scaling stage. At this last stage P&G also provided generic guidance for questions for the Growth Board should ask to counteract P&G's traditionally shorter-term focus and advance essential learning. Some of these mandatory questions were: "What did you learn? How do you know? What do you need to learn next? How can I help?"
3. **Talent and Teams:** To answer innovation questions and inform mindsets meant embarking on a continuous learning journey, starting with Kathy Fish's study and including senior leadership visits to Silicon Valley or "innovation tourism," coaching and on-the-job training of Growth Boards and involving specifically talented personnel.
4. **Metrics:** Identifying the measures that best promoted innovation was an ongoing challenge. P&G created a new metric that was closely tied to team compensation, called "entrepreneurial stewardship."
5. **Incentives:** P&G's reward process required senior level attention and advocacy, along with allocations of project funding. The need for individual rewards led to the creation of an entrepreneurial career track and changes in performance evaluation for those who chose this track.

Three pilots were conducted to demonstrate a commitment to learning by testing the theory and "putting water through the pipes." These pilots led to an organizational initiative to provide a "one-stop-shop" source called "The Garage," which guided participants into a very different way of working. The Garage offered innovators a broad range of skills that were crucial to the changes in team decision-making authority—buying media, publishing a website or fulfilling the product concept at a small scale.

In 2021 the benefits of reinvigorating this 180-year-old company were obvious when operating income jumped from $5.5 billion in 2019 to $15.7 billion in 2020. This success was attributed to a fast pivot during the pandemic, and overcoming a historically stultifying bias toward consensus through lengthy internal negotiations.[6]

## *The Work of Innovation in This Age of AI*

The adoption of artificial intelligence (AI) has captured enormous attention in the past decade, with the major inflection point being the introduction of accessible Gen AI in 2023. The emerging consensus is that AI-based innovation solutions can creatively discern inherent patterns in disparate data, while performing tasks that typically require human intelligence and learning.[7]

Early adopters such as Nestlé have seen a 60% increase in the speed of their product development activities using AI and machine learning. They got gains in the time spent on concept development, clinical data mining, process control, and early problem detection. Their experience affirms that the early benefits of AI will come through the development process lever. Possible use cases at each stage of the development process are:

*Concept generation.* This stage uses the expansive ability of Gen AI to find patterns across data sets as diverse as: trending videos, social media chatter, user forums, blogs, salesforce call reports, and internal reports. The patterns that are uncovered can reveal emerging needs and opportunities, areas that competitors are exploring, and what their customers like and dislike. AI is especially useful for finding more personalized products for hard-to-find segments. Unilever has used an AI-powered algorithm to uncover an emerging need they could meet with a new range of skin care products. Gen AI can generate novel concepts for a specific product category, but only when given the right prompts. A possible limitation is that the knowledge base is limited to events that have already happened.

Most large firms don't know what they know! Multi-divisional firms like Johnson & Johnson or Nestlé have siloed divisions with overlapping technology interests. Much of the information about possible applications of their proprietary technologies is buried in long-forgotten reports and files of their separate R&D Groups. Valuable insights can be unleashed with data mining by Gen AI; but only when the right questions are posed.

*Making the business case.* This stage applies virtually the same AI capabilities as aided concept generation, but in greater depth and hopefully greater accuracy. AI tools can scan and process multiple data sets to assess: (1) market and segment potential, (2) technology readiness and potential disruptions from other sectors, (3) competitive moves and their probable countermoves, (4) financial forecasts using different assumptions and scenarios, and (5) risk assessments and possible efforts to contain the risks, such as a building a modular facility.

Because the new AI tools can find patterns that might escape humans, forecasts of financial results should be more accurate than human forecasts, and less susceptible to the very human bias of games-playing to inflate results and make a project look more attractive than other projects competing for scarce funds. Gen AI may evolve to be like autonomous automobiles that are not sufficiently reliable to replace drivers but are reliable as co-pilots helping leaders make innovation decisions.

*Development.* AI tools will enhance the development process by: (1) Automating design tasks by rapidly creating prototypes and using predictive modeling to eliminate designs that appeal to only a few buyers, (2) Testing many iterations of virtual prototypes before they are built—some firms have found they could cut the time to develop complex components by half. Moderna uses AI to assess thousands of different mRNA-based drugs, with data-driven predictions of the best DNA sequences to test further. (3) Managing a multiplicity of projects by automating the tedious tasks of resource allocation, forecasting cashflows, and monitoring progress versus schedule, and (4) Rapidly processing unstructured feedback from product trials (in the form of recorded conversations about usage experience), to quickly surface any problems.

*Launching and learning.* Project teams can generate launch plans with AI-driven templates to streamline the planning process and then guide the sales force by automating prospect sourcing. Perhaps the biggest assistance AI will give at this stage is with setting the best price or by personalizing the pricing based on the reactions and interests of the prospective buyers.

*What's coming next?* The gains from AI advances are best realized by smart, complex, and digitally connected innovations, with software that has been thoroughly tested. One intriguing evolution is that AI will overcome previous constraints on what is possible, by enabling self-correcting new products.

## Innovation Cultures: Action or Reaction?

The cultures of growth leaders always project positive energy, optimism, and the courage to take calculated risks that encourage innovation. The reactive culture of growth laggards and their fear of failure limits their willingness to take risks. The advantages of a culture of growth leadership are on display within W. L. Gore & Associates, a mature $4.8 billion material technology company, that behaves like a start-up.[8] Gore is the antithesis of a growth laggard afflicted with slow decision-making, a bias toward efficiency and a short-term mindset.

The innovation ability of Gore flourishes within a culture that celebrates innovation and nurtures collaboration. Their culture is on display in the unique "lattice" structure of the organization of each of the four businesses (ranging from fabrics to membranes to medical products). Instead of having a hierarchy, where responsibilities are more vertical than horizontal, Gore has evolved fluid interpersonal connections where ideas and information can flow easily. There are only two roles in the company; managers who are called "leaders" and "associates." Both these roles are located in small facilities to encourage dense, cross-functional team communication. A telling observation about their leaders I have heard often is that "leaders are only leaders if someone actually wants to follow them." Leaders earn their visibility and influence by getting things done, by bringing "what's needed" together with "what's possible" with their core technology and then building a team.

One indicator of the Gore culture is what most often happens during executive team conversations about innovation. In most large companies this conversation is likely to be about how much to budget for R&D or how to balance the project portfolio. But in Gore, as the previous CEO Terri Kelly observed, the deepest conversations are about, "How do we create the right conditions where collaboration occurs naturally... where people want to work together... to be part of something greater than their individual contribution." Recruiting people to a new project, says Kelly, is a "process of giving away ownership of the idea to people who want to contribute. The project won't go anywhere if you don't let people run with it." Conversely, as one product specialist noted, "... if you can't find enough people to work on your project, maybe it's not such a good idea."

Gore is a prudent organization and taking careful, calculated risks is built into their collective DNA. Major resource commitments are made only when the key uncertainties have been addressed and action is taken to reduce their risk exposure. This posture shaped their decision to enter the market for microfiltration filters used in biopharmaceutical processing. They already sold the basic filter media into a slow growth niche market. The game changer was their innovation in membrane technology, promising a 3-fold increase in flow rates while preserving the ability to reliably catch contaminants. This made the Gore filter a superior performance alternative to traditional filters. But how should they capture and share the economic value? Many options including different pricing and distribution approaches, new routes to market and partnering models were tested with insights from potential customers, current end-users, and industry experts. It took a lot of deep digging before leadership fully embraced the business risks. The Gore culture and leadership encouraged all these challenges before deciding to launch this new business.

***Indicators of an innovative culture.*** One of the most useful indicators is how the organization deals with disappointments. A reframing of "failure" signals an opportunity to learn, correct and create something better. In the same spirit, one firm deliberately hyphenates the word *mistakes* as *mis-takes* as in "try again," to see a mistake as something to learn from and a natural part of the innovation process. Another firm replaced the word "pilot" with "pioneer" to emphasize that a pilot that may fail is supported by the full intention to keep moving ahead.[9]

Three further traits[10] or values distinguish firms with innovative cultures: First, there is a willingness to cannibalize—innovators would rather cannibalize themselves now, rather than later after their customers have migrated to a competitor offering a better solution. Second is their willingness to embrace a risk to escape the consequences of competitive defeat if they stand still. Third is their focus on the future. They are not captives of their past successes, preferring to look ahead toward their next success. Toyota reinforces this cultural value by conducting a post-mortem on each *successful* new project, to learn about opportunities to improve because they know that their customers are always dissatisfied with the existing models and ready to consider a competitor's new model.

## Leadership and Culture

The fingerprints of the leadership team are found on every facet of a culture. The overall tone is set by the top person but is magnified by the rest of the C-Suite. When the leader is the founder, it is their vision, priorities, and strength of character that have the greatest influence. Leaders populate the organization with people who respect the leader's values and exhibit patterns of behavior the leaders are comfortable with. Leaders who value innovation encourage people to take risks in pursuit of new ideas and opportunities. This gives everyone confidence that the rest of the organization will stand behind them. In contrast, operational leaders with a short-term emphasis tend to hire people who are cautious and risk averse.

When Jeff Bezos began Amazon, he shaped a culture of innovation with many powerful signals. By asking all job candidates, "Tell me about something you have invented," he signaled that innovation was expected and highly valued. He also felt strongly that some of Amazon's biggest misses came from errors of omission rather than commission. As an antidote, he encouraged his people to ask, "Why not?" when they were considering whether to develop or launch something new.

Leaders have many ways to shape the culture and reinforce their commitment to innovation as we discussed in Chapter 3. The first is how they spend their time; the more time they spend reviewing projects, working with teams, and recruiting talent, the faster their decision-making. By understanding the project better, they can identify weak signals and inflection points the project team might miss. Most companies have regularly scheduled progress review meetings—as though innovation could be scheduled. Frequent interaction outside regular meetings can speed the development activity and certainly helps leadership to ask better questions.

Most new or rapidly growing firms have a culture that is innovation friendly. But as growth slows—as it inevitably will—the firm's leadership now faces a huge cultural challenge: Will the firm continue to pursue innovation even though there is now much more to lose? Will the firm take the path of least resistance and take a more cautious stance? Will it emphasize extracting maximum economic value from its existing market position or keep a focus on growth by looking toward new markets and opportunities to be seized? A leader with an efficiency mindset is likely to drift toward M&A opportunities rather than pursuing organic growth into adjacencies and beyond. As investment and leadership attention shifts to efficiency improvements and cost cutting, the organization gets the signal, and the culture begins to ossify.

Leaders wanting to sustain their innovation culture still face a significant challenge. Rapid growth tends to weaken culture (as the pace of hiring outpaces the ability to immerse new hires into the firm's cultural norms and beliefs) and strain the existing capabilities. The competitive context is constantly changing as well. What worked in the past both internally and externally is unlikely to continue to work. Maintaining an innovation culture requires the leadership to learn to revisit the talent, capabilities, and organizational configuration regularly to assess whether they are still "fit for purpose."

## Summary: Configuring the Organization to the Work of Innovation

A healthy culture, that inspires innovation activities that are implemented with agile capabilities, can still be ineffective. The elements of culture and capability must be aligned and aimed with an organizational configuration that encourages everyone to take mindful risks and learn to improve. This configuration will answer the questions of:

- Who is accountable at the highest level for reaching the growth objective? What happens when the growth goals are missed?
- How are resources (people, investment capital, and annual budgets) allocated? What happens when resources are trapped in the core business?
- Who is responsible for identifying, selecting, and training people, and then assigning them to teams?
- How do you keep score and learn to improve? What are the key metrics in the innovation dashboard? What incentive is there for individuals and teams to meet the targets on these metrics?

These organizational questions cannot be avoided. Answers will emerge from a process of introspection about what has worked in the past, using the best insights from other firms, and by confronting the organizational inhibitors to growth. There is no set formula; the configuration that works best will be shaped by legacy factors, competitive and market realities, and the determination of leadership to improve.

Answers to these questions about configuration should be viewed through the lens of the diagnostic survey in Appendix B. The next chapter features three further ways to turn an innovation flywheel faster. The first is to approach the process of accomplishing the work of innovation by starting from the outside in; sometimes known as "working backwards." The second is to "share to gain," with an open network of collaborators with complimentary capabilities. The third is to design an innovation dashboard to guide the process of learning to improve, while ensuring that incentives and rewards push the flywheel in the right direction.

CHAPTER 8

# Turning an Innovation Flywheel Faster

When Steve Klasko began applying the four innovation disciplines the Jefferson Health System grew faster[1] than before. His initial emphasis was on hiring, promoting and developing innovation talent while improving cross-department collaboration and nurturing entrepreneurship. The new leadership of Jefferson also applied three innovation boosters that had been successfully used by other organizations, to give their innovation flywheel a further push:

- *Start from the outside in.* The hospital system held patient focus groups and town halls to better understand patient needs. This led to "hotspotting"—the strategic use of data to identify, understand, and better serve high-needs patients, so they would be less reliant on acute care settings such as emergency rooms.
- *Share to gain.* Jefferson Health partnered with IBM Watson to become the first academic medical center to join the smart hospital rooms initiative. That led to the development of a telehealth initiative called Jeff Connect. This prepared them for COVID-19 pandemic and a surge in demand for remote visits.
- *Learn and improve.* Klasko tied compensation, including his own, to innovation performance. The health system also began a variety of innovation initiatives, including naming two faculty members as "entrepreneurs in residence" and providing each with $150,000 in

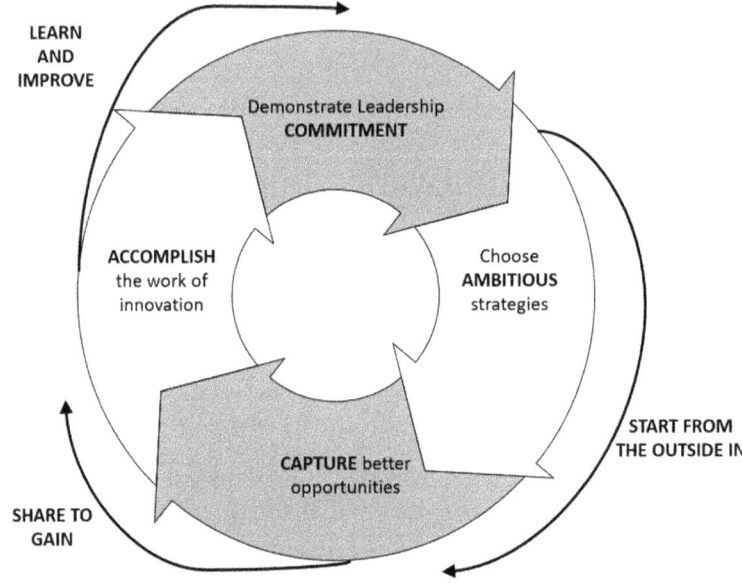

**Fig. 8.1** How innovation boosters turn a flywheel faster

funding for far-future programs, and hosting innovation hackathons with cash and business-planning prizes that attracted interdisciplinary teams from across the institution.

These three boosters accentuate the flywheel action of the innovation disciplines, as shown in Fig. 8.1.

## START FROM THE OUTSIDE IN

There is an accepted distinction between a demand-pull versus a technology-push approach[2] to innovation. This is potentially misleading because it implies an "either-or" distinction. All successful innovations emerge by iterating between these two approaches. But what really matters is which approach is used for starting the innovation process. It is demonstrably better to start with a demand-pull approach because that requires using an outside-in lens that takes the vantage points of all present and prospective customers, collaborators, and competitors. This wider lens overcomes the restricted view of the supply-push approach that starts from the inside-out by asking how the current resources, technologies, and capabilities can be applied.

A revealing contrast of the outside-in versus inside-out approaches to innovation is the choice of where to start new product development (NPD) process. Should it begin with a product or technology map that emphasizes product features and functions, or with a customer experience map that reveals the pain points and the opportunities to meet emerging or latent customer needs? A technology map narrows the scope of the innovation lens by limiting the possibilities to what is likely to be possible versus what will be needed. It risks turning the innovation process into solving a technical puzzle, rather than finding an improvement to the total customer experience. These differences can be seen in the different paths taken by Sony and Amazon to the e-book market in 2006.[3] Both the Sony eReader and the Amazon Kindle were designed to provide a better experience than printed books, at a lower cost.

When the Sony eReader was introduced, it was hailed as the iPod of the book industry. As a standalone device the eReader was exceptional: slim, lightweight, and easy to navigate. Yet a book reader is of little value without accessible and desirable content, (which the publishers were loath to provide to Sony), and a convenient process for getting e-books into the reader. Sony required the user to find, buy, and download the book file to a PC, before transferring the book from the PC to the eReader. Their inside-out focus on designing a device to use their capabilities meant they weren't attuned to the full experience of the book reader, or to meeting the needs of the ecosystem of publishers, distributors, and computer makers.

The Amazon Kindle was larger and bulkier than the Sony eReader, with an inferior user interface. However, it was much easier to connect via a wireless network and offered a vast book library. Because Amazon understood publishers, their design choices emphasized protecting the digital rights of publishers. The publishers were reassured and willing to provide their full list of books. Although Sony had a two-year head start, Amazon gained 48% of the global market by 2012 when digital books moved to the cloud.

## Why Working Backwards Works Better

Working backwards begins with the outside-in question "What's needed" before asking "What's possible." An innovation team starts the FPR/FAQ (future press release/frequently asked questions) process in Amazon by describing an innovation in customer experience as though it was ready to be launched. This description must promise a stepwise improvement in benefits to the target customers. The team also composes an accompanying "FAQ (frequently asked questions)" document which anticipates the questions leaders are likely to ask about risks, outcomes, collaboration challenges, the role of third parties, and other areas of opportunity and vulnerability.

"Working backwards" has been fully embraced by Amazon,[4] because it is supportive of three bedrock principles that Jeff Bezos built into the company from the start: customer obsession, extreme innovation, and long-term management. It applies the company's practice of gaining a deeper understanding of complex issues by using tight narratives rather than PowerPoint slides. Restricting the length of the press release to two pages forces teams to make the essence of their proposition crystal clear. The template for writing the press release requires each team to provide information about the problem it intends to solve and the opportunity it will capture, as well as explaining why existing solutions fall short.

By exposing, challenging, and testing assumptions, "working backwards" brings rigor and an outside-in discipline to the Amazon innovation process. Each of the dozens of FPR/FAQ's written each year goes through the same rigorous review process. Only a small proportion of them are funded. The review process requires the proposing team to be completely transparent and to anticipate questions. Knowing this scrutiny is ahead motivates teams to select carefully; never submitting ideas they know to be deeply flawed. They also know that they must come to the review process with a deep understanding of possible barriers or constraints that could jeopardize their proposed project and a plan to overcome them.

The working backwards approach is nurtured by externalized empathy, expressed in two of Amazon's leadership principles: "*Customer obsession.* (Leaders) work vigorously to earn and keep customer trust. Although leaders pay attention to competitors, they obsess over customers," and, "*Invent and simplify*... (Leaders) are externally aware, look for new ideas from everywhere, and are not limited by not invented here..." In his

April 2021 shareholder letter, Jeff Bezos cited a statistic showing how this kind of empathy shapes the company's decisions, "Half of all purchases on Amazon are finished in less than fifteen minutes. Compare that to the typical shopping trip to a physical store – driving, parking, searching store aisles, waiting in the checkout line, finding your car, and driving home. Research suggests the typical physical store trip takes about an hour." Amazon's leaders understand that they are really in the business of saving people time. Outsiders who discount Amazon's one-click shopping or one-day shipping overlook the importance to customers of saving their time. Amazon's empathy for its customers' needs opens up many avenues to growth, especially in financial services where querying a bank, taking out an insurance policy, or disputing a credit card charge can be frustratingly time-consuming.

## SHARE TO GAIN

The trends favoring innovation ecosystems[5] and open innovation are changing how and where the work of innovation is done. We've already seen how open innovation enhances capabilities in Chapter 3.

*Innovation ecosystems* are groups of firms with complementary activities, capabilities, and investments, coming together to create more joint value than they would have created on their own. Their whole is greater than the sum of the parts. Thus, a battery maker like Toshiba benefits by partnering with an electric vehicle maker such as Toyota.

The partners in an ecosystem are drawn together by their complementarity, although each is valuable on its own. A map and compass are useful separately but give the user much more powerful navigation guidance when they are used together. Their complementarity doesn't have to be symmetric. A software application is designed to run on an operating system, but that system does not require any specific application to be able to function. Stimulating the emergence of ecosystems is digitization that permits reconfiguration of activities and their coordination through a stable web of interactions. With boundaries between industries dissolving, there is a proliferation of interdependent—yet still independent firms—that threaten standalone companies by innovating in new directions.

The benefits of collaboration led the 1800 wine grape growers in Sonoma County, California to become the hub for a "Farm of the Future" ecosystem in 2023. These growers have long lived with the need to become more sustainable as the climate warmed. They want innovations that improve soil health, conserve scarce water, and promote biodiversity. They have recruited partners in farm equipment, agronomy, and water management to create a "living lab" for innovation, and because any solutions would need heavy front-loaded investments, they also included financing partners. The grower's organization would coordinate, facilitate, and accelerate the development of the most promising innovations. The resulting structure is shown in Fig. 8.2.

When an innovation ecosystem is controlled by a focal organization, it functions more like a private club. Managing the network for mutual benefit requires that the partners are aligned in their understanding of the

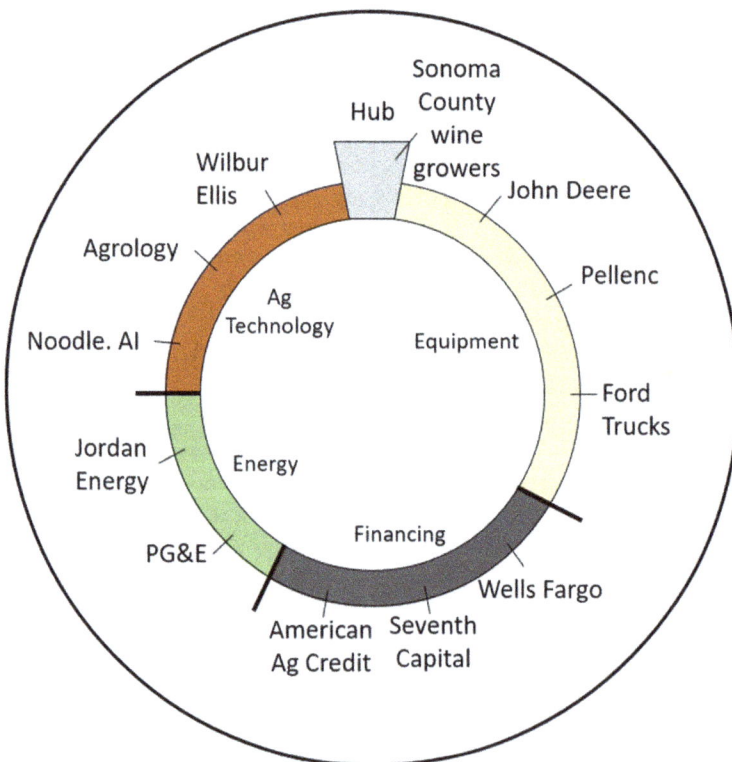

**Fig. 8.2** Farm of the future innovation ecosystem

challenges and there is a lot of mutual trust and an expectation of mutual benefits. The bringing to market of an innovation developed through an open network ecosystem poses many daunting questions to the hub organization: Which partners should we work with? How will we motivate them to collaborate? How will we keep them happy as circumstances inevitably change? How will we protect the collective intellectual property, and ensure that economic value is equitably shared? The answers will emerge if there are clear benefits to their collaboration, beyond what anyone could achieve on their own.

## Learn and Improve

This booster should measure how well a firm is innovating and indicate improvements that would turn their innovation flywheel faster. This rarely happens—few firms get the guidance they need. They are unhappy with their dashboards of innovation metrics that should tell them what needs fixing. Only 22% were "somewhat or very satisfied" with their dashboards in my survey of 192 companies. Growth leaders were not as unhappy with their dashboards and were better at using their metrics to learn and motivate their innovators.

The challenge for most firms is they will have more innovation projects to manage with tighter budgets. This balancing act requires reliable signals from an innovation dashboard. This increasing need for guidance collides with the reality that all innovation metrics are flawed proxies for what is needed and are susceptible to biases and manipulation.[6] This will not be a surprise to executives who navigate the ambiguities of innovation. I have met very few senior executives who are surprised by the disturbing results of a study (by a consortium of twelve companies) of the results of the commercialization of 120 projects that survived seven years.

The average project was forecast in support of their capital appropriation request, to breakeven in slightly less than two years. The actual performance of these projects was a median time-to-breakeven of four and a half years, with the lowest decile of projects not breaking even after six years. Why was there a lack of surprise in the gap between what was promised and what was realized? Many explanations have been suggested by these executives; the inherent optimism of innovators, the difficulty of forecasting competitive entries and counter-reactions, and the need to present a more attractive case for a share of scarce company resources than competing projects.

## Which Innovation Metrics?

Most firms are poorly served by the haphazard array of innovation metrics they use in their dashboards.[7] There are too many possible metrics without a compelling logic for choosing the best metrics. In a study of global companies I did with McKinsey, we found 58 metrics that were sorted into three sequential buckets:

- *Inputs* such as R & D spending as a percentage of sales, number of R & D projects, number of ideas or concepts in the pipeline, and the percent of ideas sourced from outside the company.
- *Process measures* that included patenting activity, percent of projects hitting their scheduled gates on time, budget versus actual spending, average time to market, and the percent of projects that are major improvements. These measures were aimed at understanding the effectiveness of the innovation processes that yielded the outcomes.
- *Performance outcomes* such as percent of sales from new products in past N years (usually 3 years), success rates, revenue growth from organic innovations, customer satisfaction, net present value of the total portfolio, and average time-to-breakeven.

Firms normally pick between 6 and 10 metrics from this menu to find a balance between too few to be useful and too many metrics causing confusion.

There was a real bias toward the use of performance outcome measures. Five of the seven most popular innovation metrics measured financial results or customer satisfaction. Outputs like revenue and profit growth due to innovations and the return on investment in innovation matter, for the promise of these results is used to justify investments in innovation. Customer satisfaction reveals the ability of the firm to create compelling offerings and please customers.

Suppose customer satisfaction with new products is poor, and the financial returns from recent innovations are disappointing? Without the insights from process effectiveness or input metrics there is no other gauge on the dashboard that will show the reason for these problems. Performance outcome measures are seldom helpful because they are lagging indicators of a long chain of decisions.

Innovation metrics that precede and influence performance have several benefits. Managers can get signals of their progress toward growth goals before a financial verdict is pronounced and the soundness of their investment decisions becomes moot. Innovators get more useful information on the actions needed to achieve the growth goals and are incented to take those actions.

Considering the lateness and lack of value from the signals given by outcome measures, why are they the most often encountered metrics in innovation dashboards? They are familiar and readily available from the management information or accounting systems. The underlying reason is not investing enough to find metrics that give useful insights into the end-to-end process of converting innovation inputs into valuable outputs. Two lessons can be drawn:

**Lesson One: Emphasize Learning Over Score Keeping:** It is essential to know whether the innovation investments and processes are delivering results. "Tailpipe measures" such as revenue and profit growth from new products, customer satisfaction, and new product success rates should certainly be included in an innovation dashboard. But these score-keeping measures won't tell you what is working or not working. Were the poor results due to inadequate or unreliable inputs, or a cumbersome and slow innovation process that stalled projects? Were too many small projects absorbing scarce resources and creating traffic jams in the development process?

The balance of metrics in the dashboard should shift toward input and process effectiveness measures. Helpful metrics will reveal loose screening that keeps too many poor ideas in the pipeline, sloppy processes that create delays, or poor quality that requires recycling the project back through development. Whirlpool Appliances uses a real-time dashboard so any innovator can tell quickly how many concepts are in process, which part of the globe they are coming from, and how many are getting close to the market. Whirlpool executives pay close attention to these metrics, because 30% of their compensation is tied to innovation performance.

**Lesson Two: Customize the Dashboard:** One size does not fit most firms and there are no "silver bullet" metrics. An innovation dashboard should satisfy three requirements; first, it fits the strategic priorities of the business and is customized for the market. What is useful for a biosciences firm with lengthy development cycles shouldn't apply to a packaged goods firm—and vice versa. Second it gives a complete picture of the entire innovation process and, third, it accepts the reality that all metrics are flawed and susceptible to gaming.

Firms should customize their innovation dashboards by choosing from a menu of metrics among the standard possibilities and then adding specialized metrics that are customized to their innovation strategy and growth goals. Most companies content themselves with the available menu approach: only 6% used measures of inputs and process effectiveness other than the ones we gave them. Compare the usual menu picking approach with the rigor that growth leaders apply to develop the metrics for their dashboards. These firms treat it as a research question and ask: Which metrics give us the most useful insights, have a demonstrable impact on business results, can be influenced by management action, and will be trusted by the organization?

Henkel, the German packaged goods giant, has adapted their dashboard to fit their market reality: many small and new products are launched each year, failure rates after launch are very high, development times are short, and competitors match any successful moves quickly. Their choices of innovation metrics were also influenced by an internal study of 2237 new products launched by themselves and four competitors over three and a half years. There were striking differences between companies in the financial returns from their new product efforts, as revealed by measures of new product share, relative number of launches (an indicator of activity, and not necessarily progress), new product launches that gained more than 1% market share, and average brand share change, which showed whether new products were building share or just replacing their existing products.

## Summary: Innovating How Innovation Works

When a firm recognizes their innovation flywheel is sluggish, leadership often succumbs to the temptation to stage an "innovation theatre" event and use it to turn the flywheel faster. A hackathon, innovation boot camp, or opportunity workshop will create short-lived enthusiasm and many ideas to pursue. These ideas overload the system and are seldom acted upon. The sense of disappointment deepens the earlier doubts about the commitment of leadership to innovation and undermines future efforts.

This dead-end story will be replayed in many other mature, slow-growing firms. But aspiring growth leaders don't wait until their growth has slowed to the pace of their markets and take pre-emptive moves. We saw this dynamic at work in the previous chapter when Proctor & Gamble leadership recognized they were being hobbled by the cautious incrementalism afflicting most mature firms and turning inward and focusing on margin improvement with cost cutting. Agile start-ups were challenging with innovative business models free of the drag of legacy thinking.

To overcome this passivity, their leadership began a multi-year change initiative. This was never going to be easy, as P&G was a large, siloed organization with rich traditions and a deeply embedded culture. Their change initiative, dubbed "GrowthWorks" is a model that others can apply, featuring closer connections of the commercial and technical functions, de-risking their investments in innovation, and changing their mindset.

P&G leaders know they will have to keep turning their innovation flywheel faster. Coming over the horizon are unprecedented changes in their markets—declining brand loyalty, new shopping habits, and a shift toward online channels. These can be opportunities if seized faster than their rivals, but will be threats if their innovation flywheel is not responsive.

# CHAPTER 9

# Sustaining a Growth Advantage

Is your firm growing faster than your rivals, and achieving its potential? Will your firm continue to grow faster?

Chances are the answers to both questions will be no. That's a problem for the leadership of slower growing firms that are 85% of the firms in most industries. These senior executives know that a credible promise of faster organic growth will raise employee satisfaction, improve recruitment, strengthen the culture and be rewarded with a stock price premium. They also know that the best innovation talent in their industry wants to join a winning team and contribute to producing better results through their efforts.

Slower growers are hindered by reactive innovation flywheels that are unable to build sustained momentum for many reasons, including:

- Episodic and weak leadership commitment to innovation and fluctuating investments in innovation talent and capabilities.
- Modest ambitions for organic growth, that become self-fulfilling prophecies.
- Tardy responses to the opportunities created by advances in technology, putting the slower growing firms farther behind the leaders who are better prepared.

Most slow growers are unhappy with their growth deficit, but don't see a path forward that doesn't jeopardize current operating profits or challenge the organizational DNA. This hesitancy may be challenged by a new leader, an unhappy board, or activist investors who urge sweeping changes to energize innovation. In response to their urging an intervention will be launched by the leadership team with much fanfare and "innovation theater"—only to be disappointed.[1] There is no "silver bullet" treatment for their slower growth that shortcuts the building of the superior innovation capabilities, structure, and systems. When the leadership team is faced with this reality, they usually revert to their past mode of reacting to the innovations of the growth leaders. This stop-start approach slows their innovation flywheel. Their immediate need for faster growth may be satisfied with the quicker fix of a big acquisition or joint venture.[2]

Committed and involved leadership is needed to turn an innovation flywheel faster through mastery of the four innovation disciplines. Success begets success: each of the four disciplines improves the more they are applied. Conversely, they can be quickly degraded by leadership neglect, complacency, overconfidence, and short-term earnings pressures. Nokia lost ground in the burgeoning smartphone market by prioritizing short-term earnings, making them reluctant to replace their aging Symbian software platform. This left Nokia unable to match the seamless customer experience of the Apple iPhone or the versatility and openness of the Android platform.

This book is a proven guide for leadership teams wanting their firms to improve how they innovate and grow faster. It presents the best current thinking and research, to answer the five crucial growth questions posed in the introduction:

1. How much faster can we grow from within?
2. Do we have the right organization?
3. How can we prepare for future growth opportunities when the present devours our attention?
4. Can a firm take a disciplined approach to innovation while encouraging exploration and creativity?
5. Can a growth laggard ever catch up to a growth leader?

In a future of relentless change and an unstoppable pace of innovation, Boards and leadership teams should put these crucial growth questions on their agendas and take informed action.

## How Much Faster Can We Grow From Within?

Superior organic growth takes dedication and resources—financial, talent, brand, capabilities—applied through an innovation flywheel. Growing faster than the industry depends on increasing the momentum of this flywheel and overcoming the "bottlenecks" that put limits and brakes on the flywheel. For most firms these constraints on organic growth are imposed by erratic leadership commitment to innovation and a consequent shortage of innovation talent.

Growth leaders are always trying to get the talent that enables faster growth, achieved by penetrating their markets more deeply or capturing opportunities in adjacent markets better than rivals. They make sustained investments in their innovation capabilities, processes, and culture to eliminate possible growth bottlenecks and turn their innovation flywheels faster.

My research and experience consistently finds that growth leaders are led by engaged and committed leadership teams who together push their innovation flywheels forcefully and steadily. The strongest indicator of their collective commitment is the time they invest in recruiting, developing, and retaining the best innovation talent. When leaders devote their scarce time to innovation talent the whole organization understands that innovation is a high priority. Two of Amazon's[3] fourteen leadership principles reinforce this point: "*Leaders are right, a lot.* They have strong judgement and good instincts. They seek diverse perspectives and work to disconfirm their beliefs," and "*Hire and develop the best.* Leaders raise the performance bar with every hire and promotion. They recognize exceptional talent and willingly move them throughout the organization…"

Three of Amazon's leadership principles encourage the pre-emptive capture of opportunities: *Invent and simplify* emphasizes the need to "look for new ideas from everywhere…" Think big asserts that "thinking small is a self-fulfilling prophecy. Leaders create and communicate bold direction that inspires results. They think differently and look around corners for ways to serve customers." The Bias for Action leadership principle says, "Speed matters in business. Many decisions and actions are reversible and do not need extensive study. We value calculated risk taking." By searching for opportunities, reimagining and stretching their entire value proposition and business model, growth leaders bring new concepts rapidly to the point they can be screened and quickly tested with small, lean experiments.

Leaders can also diagnose their real commitment to innovation by asking: "How much time do we spend thinking about the future?" If the answer is "very little," they urgently need to combat the short-termism that thwarts their innovation activities. They should also ask, "do we seek diverse inputs?" Ajay Banga,[4] the celebrated former CEO of Mastercard once answered, "diversity is essential because a group of similar people tend to think in similar ways, reach similar conclusions, and have the same blind spots..." Another revealing question is, "What are the stories about innovation successes and failures we tell around here?" These narratives are a window on the prevailing mindsets and priorities of the company and its leaders.

Leadership will get further insight with questions such as, "How confident are we that our company's organic growth goals can be met?" I found that only 28% of all firms were highly confident they could achieve their organic growth goals. The disconnect between this lack of confidence and the ambitious goals for growth often prompts a pivot toward faster-growing markets. This may be pursuing an illusion, as the boxed insert below explains, a better path is to get back to basics, and approach innovation from the market back rather the usual company-forward.

---

**The Illusion of Fast-Growing Markets**

Rapid organic growth seems easier when the market is embryonic and unsaturated, with prospects for even further rapid growth. Many firms pursue these markets because they seem more attractive than their mature markets that are dismissively viewed as stagnant. While savvy growth leaders also seek embryonic markets, they take a broader, portfolio perspective that recognizes the inherent uncertainty of their promised growth and manages them as steppingstones to capture eventually.

Markets promising fast growth are also sought by direct rivals and entrants from adjacencies that have the capabilities to exploit the opportunity. This often attracts an unsustainable glut of competitors at a rate that overshoots the long-term carrying capacity.[5] Why do so many companies enter already crowded markets? Among the reasons are" (1) the

> promise of large long-run potential, (2) the industry and its growth are well known, (3) new entrants initially find little to impede them, and (4) many entrants are initially hard to detect, causing collective surprise when these unwelcome competitors arrive. It is axiomatic in economics that every opportunity bears the seed of its own reversal. This is the "law of nemesis: Nothing good lasts indefinitely because others will want to share it."

*How to approach growth opportunities.* When the pace of advances in transformative technologies is accelerating—consider the disruptive potential of Gen AI, quantum computing, hydrogen power, or CRISPR gene editing—it seems paradoxical to advocate a market-driven approach to innovation.[6] Why do Airbnb, Rocket Mortgage, Adobe, Amazon, and 3M approach their search for growth opportunities from the market back? They apply a wider, outside-in lens to see more growth possibilities sooner than their rivals and prepare their organization to act faster on them. Because advances in technology can take many possible paths to application, they gain from a market-driven guidance system that is akin to targeting a missile. Organic growth leaders are more patient because they know that most emerging technologies will suffer through a period of disillusionment before reality sets in and expectations are aligned with what's achievable at a reasonable cost.

## Do We Have the Right Organization?

Metaphors simplify complex realities so they can be understood and managed. The flywheel metaphor represents the dynamism and sequencing of the innovation disciplines. It takes a lot of effort to get an innovation flywheel turning, but with the steady and strong application of these disciplines a flywheel builds unstoppable momentum. Another metaphor relevant to this question is that innovation organizations are like computers, with culture as their software running on the hardware of organization structure, systems, and capabilities. Whether an organization is "right," is about whether these organizational elements are aligned toward innovation.

*Capabilities* are the essential enablers of innovation leadership, as featured in Chapter 3. They also constrain which growth pathways can be pursued. Consider the specialized innovation capabilities of pharmaceutical companies, such as expertise in drug discovery, deep understanding of the intricacies of clinical testing and regulatory approval processes, and access to payers, prescribers, and providers. Few of these capabilities are transferable to adjacent health care markets such as medical devices. Their entrenched cultures also limit how they grow from within.

*Innovation cultures* have many levels and facets. At the deepest level are values expressing enduring preferences. The accessible manifestation of these values are the shared beliefs about appropriate behaviors. There are no innovative organizations with shallow or forgettable cultures. In my experience, growth leaders have several deeply held beliefs about innovation. One of these beliefs is that more can be learned from failures than successes. A failure should trigger curiosity about the reasons for the disappointment and ways to create something better. Another healthy belief is that it is better to cannibalize their current offerings with a stream of innovations, than suffer later when customers are attracted to a competitor's solution. Growth leaders embrace the risks of innovation in the belief that by understanding deeply these risks they are better equipped to contain them.

An innovation culture is not created by executive fiat. It evolves over time from the behaviors modeled and encouraged by the leadership team and reinforced by rewards and recognition. Cultures are resistant to change, as a past CEO of Sony wryly noted, "Love affairs with the status quo continue even after the quo has lost its status."

*Configuration* is an alliterative word for the structure of an organization that allocates resources effectively and defines responsibilities and governance mechanisms; including how talent is assigned, targets are set, performance is evaluated, and incentives are given. Organizational configurations emerge through introspection into what has worked or not worked in the past, what will be needed in the future, plus insights from growth leaders in other industries.

The work of innovation is done through teams with diverse and complementary expertise. They can be configured in many ways; from functional matrices managed by "lightweight" project directors with team members staying in their functional homes, to team-based structures with "heavyweight" project leaders in charge of full-time functional specialists. The best choice of configuration depends on the answers to these questions:

- Who is accountable at the highest level for reaching the growth goals? What happens when the growth goal is missed?
- How are resources (people, investment capital, and annual budgets) allocated? What happens when resources are trapped in the core?
- How do you keep score? What are the key metrics in the innovation dashboard? What incentive is there for individuals and teams to meet the targets on these metrics?
- Who is responsible for identifying, selecting, and training people, and then assigning them to teams?

*Aligning the elements.* Growth-enabling cultures, capabilities, and configurations are mutually reinforced elements, as shown in Fig. 9.1. These three organizational elements are multiplicative, because any limitation with one will afflict the other elements. Thus a dysfunctional configuration of historically separated functions won't share valuable information, and subverts collaboration.

Growth leaders strengthen their organizational alignment with an outward-oriented theme that defines their cultures, dictates which capabilities to emphasize, and determines the configuration of structure and governance mechanisms.[7] Salesforce, Inc. the cloud-based software company tightens their alignment with a laser-focus on improving their customer's success and basing their innovation activities on what will become important to their customers.

Salesforce augmented its subscription-based CRM services with an Idea Exchange platform to encourage their customers to propose new features based on anticipated needs. They also have a learning platform that engages with users through gamified training and resources, to increase their proficiency and drive further revenue growth. Every innovation is designed to make their software easier to use. The subscription-pricing model also naturally generates data on customer usage and retention—a number the company publicizes to reinforce its priority to ensure customer success.

*There is no room for complacency.* Growth leaders are constantly looking over the horizon to see what is coming and assessing whether they can stay ahead. Laggards also need to frankly assess their organizations, to learn what is holding them back. All firms should regularly assess their organizations with the diagnostic questions in Appendix B, to guide their search for improvements.

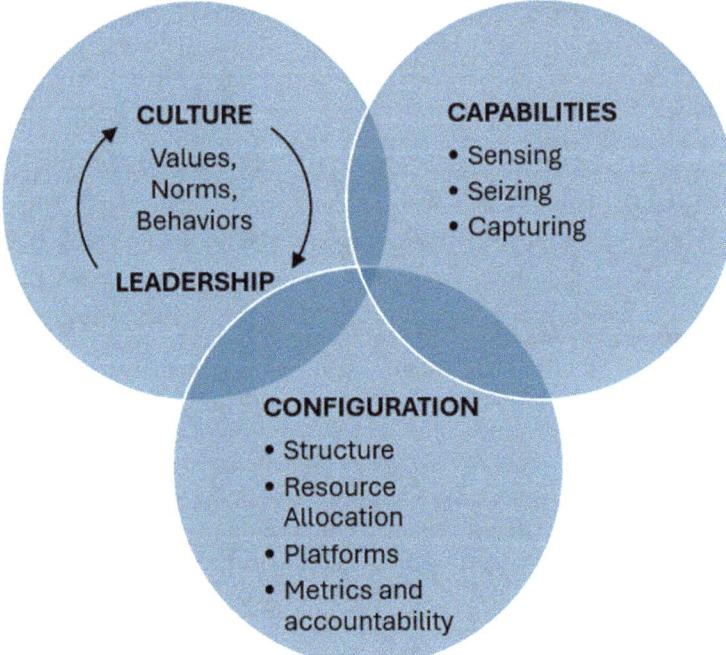

**Fig. 9.1** The innovative organization

## How Can We Prepare for Future Growth When the Present Devours Our Attention?

Growth leaders are better at simultaneously managing current operations for cash flow, to be spent on pursuing future opportunities. Growth laggards have a shorter-term emphasis on extracting economic value from their existing operations through cost cutting and efficiency gains.[8] They myopically manage for known certainties and often overlook weak signals of looming threats or potential opportunities, until they are surprised by the actions of the growth leader. Because they are forced to react, they have fewer degrees of freedom. They've lost the war for scarce innovation talent before it has begun. This compromises and slows every turn of their innovation flywheels.

Growth leaders have overcome the centripetal, inward-looking pressure of "short-termism," by balancing the inevitable tension between the exploitation of current resources and capabilities through standardization and efficiency, and the early sensing and exploration of growth opportunities.[9] They apply this knowledge by buying real options to give them flexibility to act when the time is right, and by becoming more ambidextrous.

*Ambidextrous organizations.* New ventures to explore emerging technologies and markets will operate at a different clock speed than the rest of the firm. What is needed is different configurations and cultures for the explore and exploit businesses. Microsoft used this logic to respond to Google in the corporate email and productivity markets. They appointed separate leaders for Microsoft Office to compete on the desktop and in the cloud. One unit focused on improving the customer experience, the other on moving to switch their corporate email customers to cloud-based servers. They consciously cannibalized their enterprise account business, to thwart Google. They succeeded and eventually re-combined the separate organizations into a single unit.

Advances in Gen AI have yet to improve this ambidexterity. Advances in this technology have been mainly used to improve exploitation activities by automating tasks and processes. Perhaps in the future this technology will free up time for people to focus more on the creative activities of exploration while enhancing idea generation, thus elevating and enhancing their roles and jobs.

## Can a Firm Take a Disciplined Approach to Innovation While Encouraging Exploration and Creativity?

The salience of this crucial question exposes a deeper anxiety about the possible constraining impact of tighter discipline on innovation activities. Can right-brained and left-brained activities co-exist within the same organization? Is expansive and creative thinking in conflict with the rigor and results-emphasis of a more disciplined approach?

The answer is found in the mounting evidence that most companies will benefit from healthy discipline that sharpens focus and motivates a creative search for solutions. These imposed constraints could be limits on time or money (such as mandating that fast prototyping be done by teams of five within five weeks). They can also be mandates to use certain testing protocols or design thinking methodologies, to satisfy a specific design requirement. Apple imposed the use of scratch-resistant aluminosilicate glass for the screens of their iPhone 4's and all subsequent models.

This book is a robust affirmation of the need for discipline to gain and sustain a growth advantage. Each of the four innovation disciplines applied through an innovation flywheel is a practice that an organization must master if it is to grow faster. There should be a healthy tension between the creative risk-taking and experimenting part of the innovation culture and disciplined, rigorous, and results-oriented part; an innovative organization needs both right- and left-brain functions. If one overshadows the other, performance will surely suffer. When divergent and creative thinking are encouraged by the culture, many ideas will flow but the lack of discipline in the development process means there will be too many projects competing for scarce resources. The management team also has to tolerate and encourage "well-intentioned" failures that occur for unexpected and unplanned reasons, while extracting lessons to improve the process and the next round of innovations. Without such tolerance, the people working on individual projects will avoid risks.

From an outsider's perspective, a disciplined growth leader could appear boring and predictable. On closer inspection these growth leaders are full of highly talented people who coordinate closely, and only pursue growth opportunities that fit their growth strategy and innovation capabilities. They are also better at shutting down "zombie" growth projects that absorb scarce resources and no longer advance the growth strategy.

Unless the leadership team sustains and nurtures the four disciplines, innovation activities can only react to the urging by current customers and salespeople to emphasize small-*i* projects. The antidote—advocated throughout this book—is to ensure there is a thorough understanding of the growth strategy and ambitions throughout the organization, with clear accountability for achieving the growth goals. Growth leading companies know their growth strategies need to be sold—and not just told to every employee—so each person can see how their ideas and activities can support innovation. Innovation is a team sport, and every employee is part of the team.

## Can a Growth Laggard Catch Up to a Growth Leader?

This crucial question is a thought experiment to reveal what growth leaders should prevent, and laggards should attempt. It should reveal several possible scenarios. One scenario has the growth leader losing their innovation discipline, and turning their innovation flywheel more slowly so their rivals are able to close the organic growth gap. Another scenario starts with a technological or market discontinuity the growth leader can't or won't respond to, because they are not paying attention. These scenarios are ways of learning from the future and imagining the decisions and actions that must be taken today to cope with the changes. Scenario learning identifies the possible indicators of change and vulnerability, so the firm can make pre-emptive moves.

How can this learning process help a struggling growth laggard overcome their deficiencies in innovating? The revival of KraftHeinz demonstrates what's possible with determined leadership. This story begins in 2013 when the private equity firm 3G Capital bought the stodgy condiment maker H. J. Heinz. They replaced most of the leadership team including the CEO, cut operating and innovation costs ruthlessly and consequently the patriarchal and patient culture became more transactional. The new owners then merged Heinz with Kraft Foods, the storied maker of preserved foods, to gain more leverage with suppliers and retailers. Their efficiency-oriented approach was initially vindicated when the stock rose 40% to $96.00 a share by 2017. While the market approved of their short-term moves, the discovery of the lack of growth prospects caused the stock to then drop 70% to $28.00 in the next two years.

The combined company KraftHeinz still had a portfolio of 20 strong brands—including Maxwell House, Velveeta, Kraft Cheese and Kool-Aid—that were mature and tired, but beloved by their loyal customer base. A new leadership team was hired to turn the company around with innovations in marketing and product. An early success was Heinz Remix, an internet-enabled sauce dispenser for restaurants that let their patrons blend four branded sauces to their taste. This and other innovations boosted revenues in their food service business by 14% in 2023. The stock prices responded by rising to $44.00 a share.

This story is a hopeful answer to the key issue of whether a growth laggard can become a growth leader with a strong leadership commitment to innovation. As the new CEO of KraftHeinz said in 2024, "We're going to be very disciplined in how we think about opportunities." A fitting message to conclude this book.

# Appendix A: About the Research

We used a nonsystematic sampling approach to get the benefits from gaining the full cooperation of highly placed and well-informed respondents, versus a representative sampling frame with low response rates. One difficulty in recruiting senior executives who are knowledgeable about the innovation strategies, practices, and performance of their firm (or autonomous business unit) is that even if they do agree to participate, they will frequently have a subordinate complete the survey.

Three sources were used to recruit respondents. The first source (which yielded 60% of all respondents) was a senior executive education program on innovation and strategy. Participants were prequalified as knowledgeable before their responses were accepted. The second source (20% of respondents) was participants in invitation-only innovation conferences targeting the C-Suite. The third source of a further 20% of respondents was senior leaders of companies that were partners of two major university-based research institutes. We used a combination of soft and hard copy (Qualtrics) versions of the survey as appropriate to the recruitment method. As an incentive to participate, respondents were given a chance to benchmark their company scores on all questions compared with growth leaders, laggards, and average performers.

Item development began by asking four authorities on innovation to identify potential constructs and then eliminate redundancies and ambiguities. This left 18 hypothesized drivers, which were developed into questions that were indicators of these constructs and measured on 7-point Likert (strongly agree to strongly disagree) scales. Ten of the items were reversed to minimize the biasing halo effects when all items are worded either positively or negatively. The final step in the measure development stage was to conduct two pretests of the draft survey with a total of 20 respondents. We looked for questions that elicited too many "don't know" responses and then interviewed the respondents for the purpose of clarifying the questions and eliminating and ambiguity in their wording.

The data from the 192 respondents to the survey were analyzed using bivariate correlations to assess the ability of each of the 18 hypothesized variables to explain the variance in a dependent variable measuring the organic growth rate of each company, relative to their industry peers. This dependent variable was estimated as the optimum linear correlation of three measures: *past* performance as measured by the average annual rate of organic growth of revenues in the past five years, relative to competitors: *present* spending on innovation relative to competitors; and the future was measured by the confidence of the management team that the organic growth targets in the coming three years could be achieved. There was some ecological correlation among the 18 hypothesized drivers due to the halo effect that besets all surveys, and we judged that combining the innovation drivers in multivariate regressions would obscure specific tests of our 18 hypotheses.

# Appendix B: An Innovation Diagnostic

This survey is designed for a leadership team to assess the innovation practices of their organization. The organization refers to the business unit, division, or entire firm that is the scope of responsibility.

1. **To what extent does your leadership team actively build and participate in external networks?**

   | Limited to narrow and routine industry settings (like conferences or events) | ☐ 1 | ☐ 2 | ☐ 3 | ☐ 4 | ☐ 5 | ☐ 6 | ☐ 7 | Wide engagement in diverse outside social, civic and professional networks |
   |---|---|---|---|---|---|---|---|---|

2. **What is your organizations usual attitude toward mistakes or innovation setbacks?**

   | Failure is seen as an error | ☐ 1 | ☐ 2 | ☐ 3 | ☐ 4 | ☐ 5 | ☐ 6 | ☐ 7 | Failure is seen as a learning opportunity |
   |---|---|---|---|---|---|---|---|---|

3. **How forward-looking is the strategic planning process?**

   | It is rigid, calendar-driven, and political to get access to resources | ☐ 1 | ☐ 2 | ☐ 3 | ☐ 4 | ☐ 5 | ☐ 6 | ☐ 7 | It is flexible, collaborative, issues-driven, and managed in real time |
   |---|---|---|---|---|---|---|---|---|

© The Editor(s) (if applicable) and The Author(s), under exclusive license to Springer Nature Switzerland AG 2025
G. S. Day, *Innovate to Grow*, Palgrave Executive Essentials,
https://doi.org/10.1007/978-3-031-77673-1

4. **How willing are frontline employees to forward signals of opportunities upward to the leadership team?**

| Reluctantly: We lack channels, incentives, or sufficient trust | ☐ 1 | ☐ 2 | ☐ 3 | ☐ 4 | ☐ 5 | ☐ 6 | ☐ 7 | Eagerly: We have enough trust, recognition, and incentives for doing so |

5. **How much time and resources is devote to scanning for weak signals of threats and opportunities?**

| Low priority: Few people actively watch for or examine weak signals | ☐ 1 | ☐ 2 | ☐ 3 | ☐ 4 | ☐ 5 | ☐ 6 | ☐ 7 | High priority: Many managers actively scan the periphery and explore |

6. **How are resources for innovation allocated?**

| Urgent demand from customer and the sales force absorb most of the resources | ☐ 1 | ☐ 2 | ☐ 3 | ☐ 4 | ☐ 5 | ☐ 6 | ☐ 7 | Allocations are made guided by a widely-understood innovation strategy |

7. **How diverse are the innovation project teams?**

| Teams are fairly homogenous | ☐ 1 | ☐ 2 | ☐ 3 | ☐ 4 | ☐ 5 | ☐ 6 | ☐ 7 | There is a great deal of diversity |

8. **To what extent does the leadership team demonstrate and encourage empathy for customer and employees?**

| Limited struggle to tangibly demonstrate | ☐ 1 | ☐ 2 | ☐ 3 | ☐ 4 | ☐ 5 | ☐ 6 | ☐ 7 | Significant: members demonstrate and encourage empathy |

9. **How important is innovation talent?**

| Developing innovation talent is not a priority | ☐ 1 | ☐ 2 | ☐ 3 | ☐ 4 | ☐ 5 | ☐ 6 | ☐ 7 | We invest heavily to recruit, develop and retain innovation talent |

## 10. What is the time horizon for leadership?

Emphasize efficiency and short-term (quarterly) results    ☐ ☐ ☐ ☐ ☐ ☐ ☐    1 2 3 4 5 6 7    They play a long game and invest for the future

## 11. How are anomalies in the external environment treated?

Usually ignored or met with skepticism    ☐ ☐ ☐ ☐ ☐ ☐ ☐    1 2 3 4 5 6 7    Explanations are pursued with mind-expanding hypotheses

## 12. How is the innovation strategy developed?

Inside-out: We start with our capability and technology advances    ☐ ☐ ☐ ☐ ☐ ☐ ☐    1 2 3 4 5 6 7    Outside-in: Strategy dialogue starts with customer, competitors and adjacencies

## 13. How good at gaining customer insights?

We are poor at listening to customers and anticipating their needs    ☐ ☐ ☐ ☐ ☐ ☐ ☐    1 2 3 4 5 6 7    Every leader is attuned to the "voice of the customer"

## 14. Do the leaders challenge key assumptions?

They are conventional thinkers and accept the status quo    ☐ ☐ ☐ ☐ ☐ ☐ ☐    1 2 3 4 5 6 7    They are willing to frequently challenge these assumptions

## 15. What is the process for searching for growth opportunities?

Largely undisciplined and reactive    ☐ ☐ ☐ ☐ ☐ ☐ ☐    1 2 3 4 5 6 7    Highly disciplined and systematic

# List of Figures

Fig. 2.1 Turning an innovation flywheel
Fig. 3.1 The personal competencies of effective innovators
Fig. 3.2 Innovation capabilities
Fig. 3.3 Zones of wine growing industry uncertainty
Fig. 3.4 Signaling commitment to innovation
Fig. 4.1 Elements of an organic growth strategy
Fig. 4.2 Past sources of organic growth* (*Excludes the effects of acquisitions)
Fig. 4.3 Closing the growth gap
Fig. 4.4 The innovation continuum
Fig. 4.5 The innovation risk matrix
Fig. 4.6 Different allocations for different aspirations (*Source* Nagji and Tuff [2012])
Fig. 5.1 The dimensions of a strategy to be reimagined
Fig. 5.2 Innovation avenues and pathways
Fig. 6.1 Adobe's innovation pathways
Fig. 6.2 Screening for learning
Fig. 6.3 Prioritizing assumptions
Fig. 7.1 The eight levers of a work system
Fig. 8.1 How innovation boosters turn a flywheel faster
Fig. 8.2 Farm of the future innovation ecosystem
Fig. 9.1 The innovative organization

# END NOTES TO INNOVATE TO GROW

*Chapter Two: Learning from Growth Leaders*

1. This quote came from D. Unger, "Strategy in Three Dimensions," *Strategy + Business* (May 2018), 38–45.
2. Peter F. Drucker, *Innovation and Entrepreneurship*, New York: Harper & Row, 1985 defined innovation as, "endowing human and material resources with new and greater wealth – producing capacity."
3. These two approaches are dissected further in George S. Day, "Diagnosing the Market-Driven Approach to Innovation: Learning from Practice," *Strategic Management Review* (2024).
4. The study of failure rates is described in George S. Day "Is It Real? Can We Win? Is It Worth It? Managing Risk and Reward in an Innovation Portfolio," *Harvard Business Review*, 85/12 (December 2007), 110–120. This study broadly defined "failure" as significantly missing the revenue, profitability and cash flow objectives that were used to justify the investment.
5. For other benefits of paranoia see Andy Grove, *Only the Paranoid Survive*, New York: Currency, 1996.

6. Since Edith Penrose first proposed "*The Theory of the Growth of the Firm*" (Oxford, Blackwell, 1959) the performance objective has been generally accepted to be a superior rate of organic growth in revenues and earnings. CEOs have endorsed this objective. For example, see R. Baeza et al., *The CEO Innovation Agenda*, Boston Consulting Group, 2021.
7. A look at the share price performance of 550 US and European countries over 15 years showed that for all levels of revenue growth, companies with more organic growth generated higher shareholder returns than those that relied on inorganic growth. Kabir Ahuja, Liz Hilton Segal, and Jesko Parrey, "Mastering Three Strategies of Organic Growth," New York: McKinsey & Co (August 21, 2017).
8. Juha-Antti Lamberg, Sandra Lubinaite, Jav Ojala, and Henrikki Tikkkaren, "The Curse of Agility: The Nokia Corporation and the Loss of Market Dominance in Mobile Phones, 2003–2013," *Business History*, 63 (2021), 574–605. Nokia survived and as of 2023 had over 70,000 employees.
9. These results were reported in Gerry P. Pisano, "How Fast Should Your Company Really Grow?," *Harvard Business Review* (March/April 2024). Earlier studies of sustainable rates of absolute growth conclude that the perennially outperforming company is a chimera, something that never existed at all. These are summarized in Clayton M. Christensen and Michael E. Raynor, *The Innovator's Solution: Creating and Sustaining Successful Growth*, Boston MA: Harvard Business School Publishing, 2003.
10. The flywheel concept was applied by Jim Collins in *Good to Great: Why Some Companies Make the Leap…And Others Don't*, New York: Harper Business, 2011, and further elaborated in Jim Collins, *Turning the Flywheel: A Monograph to Accompany Good to Great*, Harper Business, 2019. The flywheel concept has been extended to innovation by C. Gildehaus, D. Alfredo, E. Naidoo, and A. Poddu-turi, *Powering the Innovation Flywheel in the Digital Age*, Boston Consulting Group, 2021.
11. Lou Gerstner, *Who Says Elephants Can't Dance: Leading a Great Enterprise Through Dramatic Change*, New York: Harper Collins,

2009 turned around IBM where he found an insular culture, lumbering size and a market position that was challenged by the PC's that IBM helped introduce.

*Chapter Three: Demonstrating Leadership Commitment to Innovation*

1. While financial services companies were retrenching, BlackRock stayed on their course for growth through innovation. See, Douglas A. Ready, Linda A. Hill, and Robert J. Thomas, "Building a Game-Changing Talent Strategy," *Harvard Business Review* (January–February 2014).
2. See Jeff Dyer, Hal Gregersen, and Clayton M. Christensen, *The Innovator's DNA, Updated with a New Preface: Mastering the Five Skills of Disruptive Innovators*, Harvard Business School Press, 2019. The authors studied the habits of 25 innovative entrepreneurs and surveyed another 3000 executives to extract four discovery skills that are useful indicators for innovation leaders.
3. Laszlo Bock, *Work Rules: Insights from Inside Google That Will Transform How You Live and Lead*, Twelve, 2015.
4. The roles of dynamic capabilities for navigating uncertainty are developed further in David J. Teece, "Explicating Dynamic Capabilities. The Nature and Microfoundations of (Sustainable) Enterprise Performance," *Strategic Management Journal*, 28 (2007), 1319–1350, and David Teece, Margaret Peteraf, and Sohvi Leih, "Dynamic Capabilities and Organizational Agility: Risk, Uncertainty and Strategy in the Innovation Economy," *California Management Review*, 58 (Summer 2016), 13–35.
5. The usual definition of risk is that probabilities can be assigned to each of the possible outcomes. When there is uncertainty, this is not possible. There may be a few discrete scenarios or alternative futures that will capture the range of uncertainty. The Sonoma County Wine Growers zones of uncertainty were used to define scenarios, as described in George S. Day and Karissa Kruse, "How Vigilant Leaders Prepare for a Turbulent Future," *Strategy & Leadership* (September 2020).
6. These heuristics are sometimes (misleadingly) described as simple rules or rules-of-thumb. Rules are neither simple nor rigid but represent the cumulative and shared learning about what works and

when it works. See Kathy M. Eisenhardt and Charles B. Bingham, "Superior Strategy in Entrepreneurial Settings: Thinking, Doing and the Look of Opportunity," *Strategy Science*, 2/4 (2017), 246–257.
7. According to Liam Fahey, *The Insight Discipline: Crafting a Difference*, Chicago: American Marketing Association, 2018 an insight is "a new understanding of some facet of marketplace-change that makes a difference." He emphasizes that insights are a means to an end and not an end in themselves, but instead enable deeper thinking and yield better decisions that can actually be implemented.
8. There are many variants of the design thinking process: Lisa Carlgren, Ingo Rauth, and Maria Elonquist, "Framing Design Thinking: The Concept in Idea and Enactment," *Creativity and Innovation Management*, 25/1 (2016), 38–57, and Tom Brown, "Design Thinking," *Harvard Business Review* (June 2008), 232–38. For an expansive view of what is possible see, Roger Martin, *The Design of Business: Why Design Thinking Is the Next Competitive Advantage*, Boston, MA: Harvard Business School Press, 2009.
9. A useful source on how to conduct and apply small, fast experiments is Michael Schrage, *The Innovators Hypothesis: How Cheap Experiments Are Worth More than Good Ideas*, Boston MA: The MIT Press, 2014. He advocates giving five person teams, five weeks and $5000 to design and complete a fast experiment.
10. This example of Zillow Offers came from Rita McGrath's Flops File as reported in *Thought Sparks* (November 9, 2021).
11. For more on real options and their application to innovation processes, see: Avinash K. Dixit and R. S. Pindyck, "The Options Approach to Capital Investment," *Harvard Business Review* (May/June 1995), 105–115; Rita Gunther McGrath, "Who Learns Fastest, Wins: Lean Startup and Discovery Driven Growth," *Journal of Management* (2023), 1–21.
12. The value of agility amidst uncertainty is further developed in David Teece, Margaret Peteraf, and Sohvi Leih, "Dynamic Capabilities and Organizational Agility," *California Management Review*, 58/4 (Summer 2016), 13–35.
13. Open innovation means, "…assessing and exploiting outside knowledge while liberating external expertise for other's use."

Henry W. Chesborough "The Logic of Open Innovation: Managing Intellectual Property," *California Management Review*, 45/3 (2003), 33–58 and also *Open Innovation: New Imperative for Creating and Profiting from Technology*, Boston MA: Harvard Business School Press, 2003. The link to dynamic capabilities is made by David J. Teece, "Hand in Glove: Open Innovation and the Dynamic Capabilities Framework," *Strategic Management Review* (January 2020).
14. William Gibson is reported to have first said this in a 1993 interview on NPR. He also observed, "...that the future is not Google-able."
15. Steven Rosenbush, "Corporate Boards Tackle Oversight of Technology, Innovation," *Wall Street Journal* (May 16, 2023), reports how board level committees help firms look beyond their internal perspectives.

*Chapter Four: Strategies for Achieving Growth Ambitions*

1. Strategy definitions range from Edward de Bono, *Tactics: The Art and Science of Success*, London: Little, Brown 1984 and Henry Mintzberg's view that strategy is a pattern in stream of previous choice decisions (Henry Mintzberg, Bruce Ahlstrand and James Lampel), *Strategy Safari: A Guided Tour Through the Wilds of Strategic Management*, New York: Free Press, 1998, to Richard P. Rumelt, *Good Strategy/Bad Strategy*, New York: Crown Business 2011.
2. Kahneman and Tversky called this the *planning fallacy* to describe the general tendency of projects to overpromise and underdeliver. See Daniel Kahneman and Dan Lovello, "Timid Choices and Bold Forecasts: A Cognitive Perspective in Risk Taking," *Management Science*, 39 (1993), 17–31.
3. I've adapted this decomposition approach from Michael Treacy and Jim Sims, "Take Command of Your Growth," *Harvard Business Review* (April 2004), 127–133.
4. The concept of "cones of uncertainty" is fully elaborated by my colleague and authority on the concept of scenarios or learning from the future, Paul J. H. Schoemaker, *Advanced Introduction to Scenario Planning*, Cheltenham UK: Edward Elgar, 2022.

5. These financial considerations are beyond the scope of this book, and seldom become binding constraints on the ability of a firm to grow faster. If they might be, good places to start are Neil C. Churchill and John Mullins, "How Fast Can Your Company Afford to Grow?," *Harvard Business Review* (May 2001), or textbooks on financial management.
6. For a fuller discussion of this approach to increasing organic growth, see George S. Day, "Creating a Superior Customer-Relating Capability," *MIT Sloan Management Review*, 44/3 (Spring 2003), 77–82, and Bernard J. Jaworski and Robert S. Lurie, *The Organic Growth Playbook: Activate High-Yield Behaviors to Achieve Extraordinary Results – Every Time*, Chicago: American Marketing Association Leadership Series, 2018.
7. Sources for this Adobe Photoshop example were Sunil Gupta and Lauren Barley, "Reinventing Adobe," Case 9-514-066, *Harvard Business School* (January 20, 2015) and Paul Michelman, "Key Words for Digital Transformation: Interview of Shantanu Narayen," *MIT Sloan Management Review* (December 4, 2018).
8. This taxonomy resembles the McKinsey Three Horizons Model: Horizon 1 initiatives are short-term continuous innovations; Horizon 2 initiatives extend the firm's capabilities to new customers, or markets; Horizon 3 is the creation of new capabilities and business models to capture disruptive opportunities. Each horizon requires different focus, management, and tools. One feature of this horizon's model is the implicit assignment of a relative time to each horizon, versus representing the riskiness of these horizons. (See Mehrdad Baghai, Steve Coley, and David White, *The Alchemy of Growth: Practical Insights for Building the Enduring Enterprise*, New York: Basic Books, 2000.)
9. A good introduction to innovation portfolio management issues is Robert G. Cooper, Scott Edgett, and Elko J. Kleinschmidt, *Portfolio Management for New Products*, New York: Addison-Wesley, 1998.
10. Failure is defined as missing (by more than 35%) the original financial and market objectives used to justify the investment in the project. The results are consistent with recent surveys that place the overall failure rate of new products close to 40%. The ranges in

probabilities within the "rainbow bands" are due mainly to differences in the ability of firms to manage risk and avoid unnecessary failures.
11. See Bansi Nagji and Geoff Tuff, "Managing Your Innovation Portfolio," *Harvard Business Review* (May 2012), 67–74. Their definition of a growth leader was at least a 20% premium in their P/E ratio over peer companies.
12. These initiatives are evaluated in David Robertson, with Bill Breen, *Brick by Brick: How LEGO Reinvented Its Innovation System and Conquered the Toy Industry*, New York: Crown Business, 2013.
13. Open innovation was first advocated by Henry Chesborough, *Open Innovation: The New Imperative for Creating and Profiting from Technology*, Boston MA: Harvard Business School Press, 2003 and then endorsed by P&G in Larry Huston and Nabil Sakkab, "Connect and Develop: Inside Procter & Gamble's New Model for Innovation," *Harvard Business Review* (2006).
14. The logic for this approach to making a growth strategy comes from George S. Day, "Commentary on Formulating Strategy from the Outside In," *Long Range Planning*, 55/4 (August 2022).

*Chapter Five: Seeking Growth Opportunities*

1. K. Laursen and A. Salter, "Open for Innovation: The Role of Openness in Explaining Innovation Performance Among UK Manufacturing Firms," *Strategic Management Journal*, 35/2 (2006), 131–150 validate the benefits of a systematic approach. My survey of 192 senior innovation leaders found only 19% agree or strongly agreed that their firm's search process was systematic and engaged a broad slide of the organization or its partners.
2. Igor Ansoff, "Strategies for Diversifying," *Harvard Business Review*, 35 (1927), 113–124.
3. We have adopted the consensus definition of a competitive strategy by Raffi Amit and Chris Zott, *Business Model Innovation Strategy: Transformational Concepts and Tools for Entrepreneurial Leaders*, New York: Wiley, 2021 and Andrew Payne, Pennie Frow, and A. Eggert, "The Customer Value Proposition: Evolution, Development and Application in Marketing," *Journal of the Academy of Marketing Science*, 45 (2017).

4. Useful sources on the application for design thinking that highlight the role of empathy are Tom Brown, "Design Thinking," *Harvard Business Review* (2008), 232–238 and Roger Martin, *The Design of Business: Why Design Thinking Is the Next Competitive Advantage*, Boston, MA: Harvard Business School Press, 2009.
5. The stream of research in lead users is summarized in Eric von Hippel and S. Kaulartz, "Next Generation Consumer Innovation Search: Identifying Early-Stage Need Solution Pairs on the Web," *Research Policy*, 49 (2020), 23–30.
6. This example is based on a McKinsey & Company study of the wellness industry, as reported in Anna Pione, "The Trends Defining the Wellness Industry," *McKinsey Quarterly* (February 2024).
7. Useful tools for overcoming the barriers to nonconsumption are found in Scott D. Anthony, Mark W. Johnson, Joseph V. Sinfield, and Elizabeth J. Altman, *The Innovator's Guide to Growth: Putting Disruptive Innovation to Work*, Boston, MA: Harvard Business Press, 2008.
8. Chan Kim and Renée Mauborgne, *Blue Ocean Strategy Expanded Edition: How to Create Uncontested Market Space and Make the Competition Irrelevant*, Cambridge, MA: Harvard Business School Press, 2014.
9. There is a close affinity between the organic growth leaders featured in this book and vigilant organizations with superior foresight, described in George S. Day and Paul J. H. Schoemaker, *See Sooner/Act Faster: How Vigilant Leaders Thrive in an Era of Digital Disruption*, Boston, MA: MIT Press, 2019.
10. In 2006 Curves Fitness Center was the largest franchised operator of women's fitness centers in the USA It has since declined to about 300 franchises with the same value proposition per Wikipedia (accessed in 2024).

*Chapter Six: Capturing Better Opportunities*

1. These cognitive biases are well described in Daniel Kahneman, *Thinking Fast and Slow*, New York: Farrar, Straus and Giroux, 2011.
2. There are other ways to find the best growth opportunities. An innovation tournament is a variation of crowd sourcing, using

informed insiders to generate and evaluate growth opportunities created in response to a specific strategic challenge. See Christian Terwiesch and Karl T. Ulrich, *Innovation Tournaments: Creating and Selecting Exceptional Opportunities*, Boston: Harvard Business Press, 2009. A complementary tool is discovery-driven planning that is useful to reduce the assumption-to-knowledge ratio. Rita Gunther McGrath and Ian C. MacMillan, *Discovery-Driven Growth: A Breakthrough Process to Reduce Risk and Seize Opportunity*, Boston, MA: Harvard Business Press, 2009.

3. Heuristics have been studied from two directions. The original *heuristics* and *biases* perspective was central to the pioneering research of Daniel Kahneman and Amos Tversky and well described in Daniel Kahneman, *Thinking Fast and Slow*, New York: Farrar, Straus and Giroux, 2011. They defined a heuristic as, "a simple procedure that helps find adequate, though often imperfect answers to difficult questions." Their emphasis was on the bounded rationality of decision makers and the resulting complications of attention, memory and comprehension that lead to violations of the principles of rational choice. The subsequent fast-and-frugal perspective takes a more positive view of heuristics as "ecologically rational" and focuses on their utility in uncertain situations (G. Gigerenzer, "Why Heuristics Work," *Perspective on Psychological Science*, 2/1 (2008), 20–29).

4. Kathy M. Eisenhardt and Charles B. Bingham, "Superior Strategy in Entrepreneurial Setting: Thinking, Doing and the Look of Opportunity," *Strategy Science*, 2/4 (2017), 246–257.

5. These heuristics or simple rules are further discussed in George S. Day, "Capturing Innovation Opportunities: Learning from Growth Leaders," *Journal of Product Innovation Management* (June 2024), 724–734.

6. I've used this screening method with many clients, as described in my article, "Is It Real? Can We Win? Is It Worth Doing? *Harvard Business Review* (December 2007), 3–13. Other useful opportunity assessment approaches are by Eric Ries, *The Lean Startup: How Today's Entrepreneurs Use Continuous Innovation to Create Radically Successful Businesses*, New York: Crown Books 2011, and Alexander Osterwalder, Yves Pigneur, Y. Bernarda, and A. Smith, *Value Proposition Design*, New York: Wiley, 2014.

7. Scott D. Anthony et al., *The Innovator's Guide to Growth: Putting Disruptive Innovation to Work*, op. cit.
8. Avinash K. Dixit and Robert S. Pindyck, "The Options Approach to Capital Investments," *Harvard Business Review* (May/June 1995), 105–115.

*Chapter Seven: Accomplishing the Work of Innovation*

1. Useful sources were David Robertson with Bill Breen, *Brick by Brick: How LEGO Reinvented Its Innovation System and Conquered the Toy Industry*, New York: Crown Business 2013; Trevor Moss, "How Lego Beat Barbie and Monopoly," *Wall Street Journal* (March 7, 2023) and Michela Beretta, Linus Dahlander, Lars Frederiksen, and Arne Thomas, "Lego Takes Customer's Innovations Further," *MIT Sloan Management Review* (September 12, 2023).
2. Insightful diagnoses of innovation narratives are found in Caroline A. Bartel and Raghu Garud, "The Role of Narratives in Sustaining Organizational Innovation," *Organization Science*, 20 (January 2009), 107–117; Sheldon Buckler and Karen Anne Zien, "The Spirituality of Innovation: Learning from Stories," *Journal of Product Innovation Management*, 13 (September 1996), 391–405. This discussion draws on George S. Day and Gregory P. Shea, "Grow Faster by Changing Your Innovation Narrative," *MIT Sloan Management Review* (Winter 2019), 2–8.
3. The Work Systems approach draws on systems theory and was developed by Gregory P. Shea and Cassie A. Solomon, *Leading Successful Change: 8 Keys to Making Change Work*, Philadelphia, PA: Wharton School Press, 2020. We collaborated to adapt the Work System model to innovation activities, leading to our article, George S. Day and Gregory P. Shea, "Changing the Work of Innovation: A Systems Approach," *California Management Review*, 63 (Fall 2020), 41–60. We featured in this article, the story of the Whirlpool innovation model that enabled them to escape a commodity trap, based on Nancy Tennant Snyder and Deborah L. Duarte, *Unleashing Innovation: How Whirlpool Transformed an Industry*, San Francisco: Jossey-Bass, 2008.
4. A cautionary tale is told by Anna Canato, Davide Ravasi and Nelson Phillips, "Coerced Practice Implementation in Cases of

Low Cultural Fit: Cultural Change and Practice Adaptation During the Implementation of Six Sigma at 3M," *Academy of Management Journal*, 56 (December 2013), 1724–1753.
5. This section was adapted from George S. Day and Gregory P. Shea, "Innovating How Innovation Works at Proctor & Gamble," *Strategy & Leadership*, that drew from Emily Truelove, L.A. Hill and Emily Tedards, "Kathy Fish at Proctor & Gamble: Navigating Industry Disruption by Disrupting from Within," Harvard Business School Case 9-421-021 (2020).
6. Barbara Bukovac, "Procter & Gamble's Path to Constructive Disruption," *Strategy + Business* (August 4, 2021).
7. Useful sources on prospects for AI were Roberto Verganti, Luca Vendraminelli, and Marco Iansiti, "Innovation and Design in the Age of Artificial Intelligence," *Journal of Product Innovation Management* (March 2020), and Robert G. Cooper, "The Artificial Intelligence Revolution in New Product Development," *IEEE Engineering Management Review*, 52 (February 2024), 195–211.
8. Sources of information on W. L. Gore & Associates include multiple interviews of senior leaders, observations based on long relationships with the company and observers such as Gary Hamel who featured the company in the *Future of Management*, Boston: Harvard Business School Press, 2007.
9. Laura Fursenthal, "Taking Fear out of Innovation," an episode of the *Inside the Strategy Room* podcast by McKinsey & Co (March 2023).
10. Based on a study of 770 companies across 15 countries by Gerard J. Tellis, *Unrelenting Innovation: How to Create a Culture for Market Dominance*, San Francisco, CA: Jossey-Bass, 2012.

*Chapter Eight: Driving an Innovation Flywheel Faster*

1. This analysis of Jefferson Health is based on research reported in George S. Day and Gregory P. Shea, "Grow Faster by Changing Your Innovation Narrative," *MIT Sloan Management Review* (Winter 2019), 2–7. By 2024 this hospital system reported a loss of $78.5 million from operations on revenue of $9.7 billion. In common with most other hospitals nationwide they have struggled

with rising costs since the pandemic and had to pay further costs to service the debt they incurred in acquiring other hospital systems.
2. This distinction has a long history (David C. Mowery and Nathan Rosenberg, "The Influence of Market Demand Upon Innovation: A Critical Review of Some Recent Studies," *Research Policy*, 8 (1979), 102–153) and remains widely used (for example, see L. Chaston, *Technological Entrepreneurship: Technology-Driven vs Market-Driven Innovation*, New York: Palgrave Macmillan, 2017, as a handy way to simplify and communicate the diversity of innovation approaches).
3. This example was derived from Ron Adner, *The Wide Lens: A New Strategy for Innovation*, New York: Penguin, 2012.
4. "Working backwards" is described in Colin Bryar and Bill Carr, *Working Backwards: Insights, Stories and Secrets from Inside Amazon*, New York: St. Martin's Press, 2021, and John Rossman, *The Amazon Way: Amazon's Leadership Principles*, New York: Clyde Hill Publishing, 2021. I've combined these sources with my own interviews within Amazon in a broader context and contrasted "working backwards" with the familiar stage-gate processes in George S. Day, "Why Working Backwards Works Better," *Management and Business Review*, 2 (Spring 2022), 1–7.
5. An introduction to ecosystems is Marcus Holgersson, Carliss Y. Baldwin, Henry Chesbrough, and Marcel Rogers, "The Forces of Ecosystem Evolution," *California Management Review*, and its special section on Ecosystems and Open Innovation in the same issue (Spring 2022), 5–23.
6. For insights into these biases, especially the availability and survivorship biases, see Michael Harris and Bill Tayler, "Don't Let Metrics Undermine Your Business," *Harvard Business Review* (September–October 2019), 63–69.
7. This section on innovation metrics draws on my white paper for the Mack Institute for Innovation Management at the Wharton School, *Metrics for Managing Innovation: Lessons from Growth Leaders* (Fall 2020).

*Chapter Nine: Sustaining a Growth Advantage*

1. Gerry Myers, VP Global Innovation of Chubb & Son calls this an "Innovation Carnival" that starts with "let's set up a

skunkworks…build an innovation dashboard…hold an innovation tournament…co-create with customers…embrace open innovation…" These episodic interventions don't address systemic failings, and fly in the face of innovation as an always on, collaborative activity engaging everyone.
2. Peter Drucker (*Managing for the Future*, New York: Dutton, 1992, page 160) felt that the impulse for acquisitions came less from sound reasoning and more because doing deals is more exciting than doing the disciplined work of innovation.
3. There are many insider books about Amazon. Two recent publications that I also used in Chapter 8 are Colin Bryar and Bill Carr, *Working Backwards: Insights Stories and Secrets from Inside Amazon*, New York: St. Martin's Press, 2021 and John Rossman, *The Amazon Way: Amazon's 14 Leadership Principles*, New York: Clyde Hill Publishing, 2021.
4. Ajay Banga was President and CEO of Mastercard from 2010 to 2021. During his tenure, Banga tripled revenues and increased net income sixfold. He became President of the World Bank in 2023.
5. Few growth industries (perhaps including the burgeoning AI industry) are exempt from the wrenching failures and thwarting of aspirations that accompany a shakeout. For my diagnosis of the reasons and prescriptions for survival, see George S. Day, "Strategies for Surviving a Shakeout," *Harvard Business Review*, 75 (March–April 1997), 92–102.
6. Being market-driven emphasizes the need to be "relentlessly compelled" by market realities and opportunities for growth, as implied by the dictionary meaning of "driven." The term is intended to be broader than customer-led or customer-centric, to address the concerns of Clayton Christensen (*The Innovator's Dilemma: When New Technologies Cause Great Firms to Fail*, Boston: Harvard Business School Press, 1997) and others, that firms should not be myopically focused on satisfying their current profitable customers, and pay closer attention to potential customers in embryonic but growing markets that could support new concepts.
7. For a deep but dated dive into the complexities of innovation governance, see Jean-Phillipe Deschamps and Beebe Nelson, *Innovation Governance: How Top Management Organizes and Mobilizes for Innovation*, Jossey-Bass, 2014.

8. Growth laggards unfortunately share many attributes of the vulnerable organizations I have studied with my colleagues Paul Schoemaker, *See Sooner/Act Faster: How Vigilant Leaders Thrive in an Era of Digital Turbulence*, Boston: MIT Press, 2019.
9. This distinction was first formalized by James G. March, "Exploration and Exploitation in Organizational Learning," *Organization Learning*, 2 (February 1991), 71–87. The balancing of these capabilities has been an ongoing issue: see Julian Birkinshaw and Cristina Gibson, "Building Ambidexterity into an Organization," *MIT Sloan Management Review* (July 15, 2004), and Charles A. O'Reilly and Michael L. Tushman, "Organizational Ambidexterity in Action," *California Management Review*, 53 (Summer 2011), 5–23.

# Index

**A**
Accountability, 20
Activator Corp, 39, 40
Adjacencies, 9
Adjacent geographies, 61
Adobe, Inc., 39, 47, 72, 73, 111
Adobe Photoshop, 47, 72
Adoption-chain risk, 36
Agility, 32, 34, 60, 81, 92
Airbnb, 7, 111
Aladdin, 23
All in Motion, 61
Allocations, 18
Amazon, 10, 33, 38, 91, 97–99, 109, 111
Amazon Kindle, 97
Ambidexterity, 115
Ambidextrous organizations, 115
Ambitions, 18, 19, 41
Analytical frameworks, 69
Anchoring, 70
Android, 108
Ansoff matrix, 56
Apple, 10, 60, 108, 116
Approaches, 19
Approach their present, 29
Arenas, 19, 50
Artificial intelligence (AI), 6, 87–89
 tools, 88
Average performers, 13

**B**
Banga, Ajay, 110
Beyond Meat, 9
Bezos, Jeff, 91, 98, 99
Bias, 88
BIG I growth initiatives, 51
BIG-I innovation, 9, 19, 34, 35, 47, 49
Biogen, 38
Biotech, 34
BlackRock, 23
Blue Ocean Strategy, 62
Bohr, Niels, 44

Brakes, 21
Business case, 88
Business Model (BM), 56, 65, 67

**C**
Cannibalize, 90, 112
Capability(ies), 36, 37
　assessments, 38
　development, 38
Cargo drone, 6
Casper Sleep, 44
Castrol Industrial, 67
Chat GPT, 28
Chief human resources officer (CHRO), 25, 27
Churn rate, 43
Cisco, 12
Cloud-based storage, 72
Cloud computing, 72
Cognitive biases, 69
Collaboration, 20
Collective curiosity, 17
Collective intelligence, 70
Comcast, 67
Competitive advantages, 10, 27
Competitive strategy, 56
Complainers and defectors, 31, 59
Complementarity, 99
Complete solutions, 63
Concept generation, 87
Conceptual thinking, 26
Configuration, 112, 113
Confirmation bias, 70
Constraints, 51
Consumer packaged goods, 72
Consumption, barriers to, 61, 62
Convergence, 68
Core business, 21
Corning Inc., 71
Corporate innovation fund, 50
Creativity, 8

CRM, 113
Culture(s), 20, 81, 89–92, 111, 112, 115
Curiosity, 26
Curves Fitness Center, 68
Customer experience, 63
Customer journey, 46
Customer-oriented categories, 42
Customer segment, 46, 61, 65
Customer value leadership, 56
Customer Value Proposition (CVP), 56

**D**
Danaher, 13
Dashboard(s), 101–104
Decomposition, 42
DeepMind lab, 28
Defect, 45
Demand-pull approach, 96
Design thinking, 30, 57, 115
Development process, 87, 88
　phase-gate, 34
　stage-gate, 34
Diagnostics firms, 72
Diffused knowledge, 60
Digital physician engagement platform, 74
Disappointment(s), 9, 31, 32, 90
Disciplined work, 8
Discovery skills, 25, 27
Divergence, 68
Dow Corning, 74
Dynamic capabilities, 27

**E**
Economic returns, 19
Ecosystem, 7, 99
Efficiency gains, 8
Efficiency mindset, 91
Elements of value model, 59

Emerging technologies, 111
Empathy, 98, 99
Entrepreneurial career track, 86
Entrepreneurial stewardship, 86
Experimental approach, 33
Experimental mindset, 32
Experimentation, 25, 85
Exploratory options, 34
Extracting, 91

**F**
Failure(s), 31, 90, 110, 112
FAQ (frequently asked questions), 98
Farm of the Future, 99
Fast and frugal heuristics, 71
Fast-to-fail, 86
Filters, 70
Financial analysis, 69
Fish, Kathy, 85, 86
Flow of ideas, 8
Ford, 32
Forecast, 33
Foresight, 10
FPR/FAQ process, 98
Friction-reduction technology, 65

**G**
Gamesmanship, 70
Garage, The, 86
Gatekeepers, 35
Generative AI, 10, 17, 27, 28, 35, 38, 44, 46, 51, 59, 60, 67, 87, 88, 111, 115
Gibson, William, 38
Ginger budget hotel chain, 62
Globalization, 61
Google, 27, 28, 47, 72, 115
Go-to-market approach, 66
Governance, 86
Groupthink, 70
Grove, Andy, 10

Growth advantage, 107
Growth Board, 85, 86
Growth gap, 42, 45, 46, 49
Growth goals, 5, 18, 34, 41, 42, 45, 49, 81, 82, 92, 103, 104, 110, 113, 116
Growth initiatives, 42
Growth laggards, 7, 9, 12, 30
Growth leaders, 12, 16, 24, 29, 32
Growth opportunities, 18, 55, 69, 111
Growth pathways, 68
Growth strategy, 18, 39–41, 50, 53
GrowthWorks, 105

**H**
Haier, 36
Hasbro, 82
HBO, 67
Heinz Remix, 117
Henkel, 104
Herman Miller, 78
Heuristics, 19, 70, 71, 75, 79
Hotspotting, 95

**I**
IBM, 47
IBM Watson, 95
Idea Exchange platform, 113
IDEO design consultancy, 31
Impossible Foods, 9
Incremental improvements, 7
Incumbents curse, 14
Industry life cycle, 13
Inherent uncertainty, 32
Inhibitors, 20
Innovation, 6, 40
  aspirational, 7
  future forward, 9
  incremental or small, 8
  iterative, 8

seizing, 31
Innovation activities, 36
Innovation advantage, 25
Innovation brokers, 36
Innovation capabilities, 27, 28, 112, 116
Innovation competencies, 26
Innovation culture, 92, 112
Innovation dashboard(s), 16, 101, 103
Innovation disappointments, 29
Innovation discipline(s), 5, 8, 13, 15–18, 21, 85, 95, 96, 108, 111, 116, 117
Innovation ecosystem, 99, 100
Innovation failures, 31
Innovation flywheel(s), 5, 6, 16, 17, 20, 21, 28, 37, 95, 101, 104, 105, 107–109, 111, 114, 116, 117
Innovation initiatives, 31, 47, 68
Innovation leaders, 14, 24
Innovation leadership role, 26
Innovation metrics, 20, 101, 102
Innovation narrative, 82, 83
Innovation opportunities, 69
Innovation portfolio, 47, 49
Innovation processes, 27, 50, 52
Innovation project, 25
Innovation risk matrix, 47
Innovation talent, 18, 23–25, 36, 107, 109
Innovation tax, 50
Innovation theater, 108
Innovative imitation, 60
Innovative talent, 27
Innovative work practices, 81
Inputs, 102
Inside-out approach, 8, 42, 53
Insight seeking, 29
Intuit, 74, 75
Invention, 7

Investors, 11
iPhone, 7, 60, 108, 116
iPod, 60

**J**
Janssen (Pharmaceuticals), 36
Japanese companies, 7
Jeff Connect, 95
Jefferson Health System, 95
Jefferson University, 83
Job rotation, 27
Johnson & Johnson, 13, 87
Joint ventures, 14
Just-in-time systems, 65

**K**
Klasko, Dr. Stephen, 83
Klasko, Steve, 95
KraftHeinz, 117

**L**
Lafley, A. G., 52
Laggard, 28
Latent customer needs, 57
Latent market needs, 29, 30
Launching, 88
Leaders, 89
Leadership commitment, 5, 7, 15, 17–21, 23, 27, 37, 107, 109, 117
Lead users, 31, 59
"Leaner" gates, 35
Learn and improve, 95
Learn from their past, 29
Learning, 9, 103
Learning platform, 113
LEGO Group, 7, 51, 71, 81, 82
LEGO Ideas platform, 52, 81
LinkedIn, 37

## M

Maersk Line, 66
Market back, 110, 111
Market-driven approach, 111
Market opportunities, 74, 75
Mastercard, 110
Mattel, 82
McDonald's, 47
McKinsey, 102
Meat substitute, 9
Medtronic, 34
Metrics and incentives, 20, 102, 104
Microsoft, 38, 47, 72, 115
Microsoft Office, 115
MightyFly, 6
Moderna, 88
Momentum, 6
Momentum curve, 45
Momentum forecasting, 43–45

## N

Narrative, 13
NASA, 35
Nestlé, 87
Netafim, 67
Networking, 25
New futures, envisioning, 29
New product development (NPD), 97
Nike, 66
Nokia, 12, 108
Novartis Pharmaceuticals, 73, 74
Novo Nordisk, 39

## O

Observing skills, 25
Omnichannel, 67
Open AI, 28
Open innovation, 36
Operating culture, 24
Operational leaders, 91
Opportunities
 capturing, 5, 19
 emerging, 21
 screening of, 76
Opportunity-capturing heuristics, 71
Opportunity horizon, 30
Ordinary capabilities, 27
Organic growth, 11, 40, 109–111
Organic growth leaders, 14
Organic growth rate, 46
Organizational configuration, 92, 112
Organizational frictions, 17
Outside-in approach, 8, 53, 95, 96, 111
Outside-in view, 64
Overconfidence, 70

## P

Partners, 11–14, 17, 20, 23, 32, 36, 38, 40, 47, 52, 65, 99–101
Partnerships, 14
Past growth, 42
Performance outcomes, 102
Peripheral vision, 64
Personal competencies, 26
Personalization, 60
Personalized products, 87
Pilots, 78, 86
Pinkberry, 64
Platform business models, 66
Postmortem, 49, 70, 90
Praxair, 67
Precursors, 31, 59
Preserve and protect options, 34
Pret A Manger, 62
Probe-and-learn-mindset, 33
Process measures, 102
Proctor & Gamble (P&G), 52, 85, 86, 104, 105
Product escapes, 39
Product-sale model, 67
Project portfolio, 89

Prototype, 30, 57
Prototyping, 77
Pull of the market, 6
Push of technological possibilities, 6

**Q**
Quantification of fantasy, 45
Questioning, 25
QuickBooks, 74

**R**
Reactive approach, 19, 55, 68
Reactive firms, 51
Readiness advantage, 78
Real options, 32–34, 70, 78, 115
Relative growth, 13
Research & development (R&D), 8
Resource allocation, 38, 69, 70
Risk, 20
  avoidance of, 8
  degree of, 8
Risk-based contracts, 63
Rocket Mortgage, 111
Routinizing innovation, 85

**S**
"Safe" projects, 49
Salesforce, Inc., 113
Scanning the periphery, 28, 29
Scenario planning, 65
Scenarios, 29
Scope, 51
Scouting options, 34
Screening, 55, 77
  framework, 70, 75
  process, 76
Searching, 55
Seizing, 27
Selecting, 55
Sensing, 27, 28

Sephora, 9
Served markets, 61
Share to gain, 95
Short-termism, 114
Simple rules, 19
Six Sigma, 85
Small $i$ initiatives, 49
Small-$i$ innovation, 19, 35, 47, 49, 50, 116
Sonoma County Wine Growers, 29, 99
Sony, 97, 112
Sony eReader, 97
Sophos, 63
Starbucks, 17
Stop-start approach, 108
Subscription model, 67
Symbian, 108
Systematic approach, 68
Systematic search, 55

**T**
Tailpipe measures, 103
Talent, 15
Talent scouting and recruiting, 37
Talent war, 24, 27
Target Stores, 60
Tata Group, 62
TCBY ("The Country's Best Yogurt"), 64
Technology, advances in, 59, 66
Technology-push approach, 96
3G Capital, 117
3M Company, 31, 111
Toehold investments, 78
Toshiba, 99
Toyota, 99
Transformative technologies, 111
Turbulence, 21

## U
Uber, 62, 66
Uncertainty, 14
　cone of, 44
　zones of, 29
Unilever, 87
User-centeredness, 30

## V
Value-capture system, 67
Value-creating activities, 65
Value profile, 62
Value proposition, 57
Vigilant learning, 64

## W
Walmart, 39
Warby-Parker, 61
Wellness market, 60
Westin Hotels, 64
"What if" scenarios, 35
Whirlpool Appliances, 103
Wide-spectrum approach, 56
Wide-spectrum framework, 19
W. L. Gore & Associates, 89
Work environment, 84
Working backwards, 98
Work of innovation, 5, 15, 19, 20, 23, 81, 82, 84, 85, 87, 92, 99, 112

## X
Xerox, 47
XIAMETER, 74

## Z
ZARA apparel chain, 65
Zillow, 33
Zillow Offers, 33

GPSR Compliance

The European Union's (EU) General Product Safety Regulation (GPSR) is a set of rules that requires consumer products to be safe and our obligations to ensure this.

If you have any concerns about our products, you can contact us on

ProductSafety@springernature.com

In case Publisher is established outside the EU, the EU authorized representative is:

Springer Nature Customer Service Center GmbH
Europaplatz 3
69115 Heidelberg, Germany

www.ingramcontent.com/pod-product-compliance
Lightning Source LLC
LaVergne TN
LVHW010342260326
834688LV00036B/846